Promoting
RIGOR
Through HIGHER
LEVEL
QUESTIONING

Promoting
RIGOR
Through HIGHER
LEVEL
QUESTIONING

Practical Strategies for Developing
Students' Critical Thinking

TODD STANLEY

PRUFROCK PRESS INC.
WACO, TEXAS

Library of Congress Control Number:2019952164

Copyright ©2020, Prufrock Press Inc.

Edited by Katy McDowall

Cover design by Allegra Denbo and layout design by Raquel Trevino

ISBN-13: 978-1-61821-899-5

Printed in the United States of America.

At the time of this book's publication, all facts and figures cited are the most current available. All telephone numbers, addresses, and website URLs are accurate and active. All publications, organizations, websites, and other resources exist as described in the book, and all have been verified. The authors and Prufrock Press Inc. make no warranty or guarantee concerning the information and materials given out by organizations or content found at websites, and we are not responsible for any changes that occur after this book's publication. If you find an error, please contact Prufrock Press Inc.

Prufrock Press Inc.
P.O. Box 8813
Waco, TX 76714-8813
Phone: (800) 998-2208
Fax: (800) 240-0333
http://www.prufrock.com

TABLE OF CONTENTS

Introduction
Rating Your Questioning Behavior

Essential Question

How do you rate your questioning behavior?

Every year, teachers and schools across the world pay millions of dollars for curriculum in order to challenge their students, in the form of textbooks, computer programs, prescribed lessons, modules, projects, etc. Teachers use these programs to promote rigor in the classroom and higher level thinking in their students. Educators want to challenge all of their students, from their gifted and high-achieving students to their lower achievers, and will pay top dollar to do so. Of course, what the makers of these products are not going to tell you is that you do not have to purchase these wares, nor do you have to spend all that money, in order to challenge your students. Just like Dorothy and her red slippers, you have had the power the entire time—and it does not cost anything.

What is this magical superpower that lies within you? Do you have to come across an alien spacecraft, be exposed to gamma rays, or be bitten by a radioactive spider in order to access it? No. This power is actually something teachers do every single day with their students; it is the power of questioning. How you can challenge your students day in and day out, raising the rigor of your classroom to meet the needs of all of your students, comes down to one factor: What questions are you asking?

Keep in mind that not all questions are created equally. There are questions that are well asked and promote critical thinking. Then, there are questions that accomplish nothing other than canned or yes-or-no responses that do not elicit deep thinking from the respondent. People always are saying, "I know this is a stupid question, but . . ." and the obligatory response is that there are no "stupid" questions. I am here to tell you that there is such a thing—especially in the classroom where you are trying to build the thinkers of tomorrow. As a matter of fact, all sorts of "stupid" questions can actually do much more harm than good. And, unfortunately, these questions are asked daily in classrooms all across the world.

At this point you are probably starting to get a little anxious, wondering whether you are a teacher who is asking "stupid" questions. The good news is that every teacher is guilty of asking a "stupid" question from time to time, but the bigger picture question is: Do you recognize when ineffective questions are asked? Some teachers might think that the questions they are asking are effective, discovering, only under further scrutiny, that they are not the type of questions that improve student learning. Figure 1 outlines the differences between good questions and bad questions.

To help determine how the questions in your classroom are impacting the learning and understanding of your students, I would like you to do a self-evaluation. Now, keep in mind, self-evaluations only work if you are honest with yourself. In

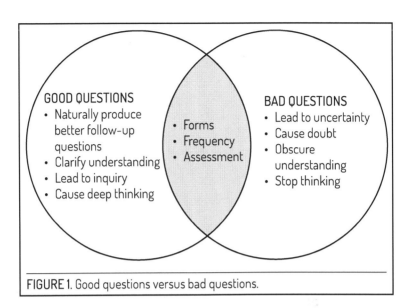

FIGURE 1. Good questions versus bad questions.

some ways, you are better off being harsher on yourself during a self-evaluation. The good news is that the only person who is going to see the evaluation is yourself, so there is nothing preventing you from being completely forthcoming. You are going to answer the following 10 questions as best you can, using a scale of 1–5 (1 being you do the indicated activity very poorly, and 5 being you do it at an expert level). Just for the record, although I thought I was pretty good at asking rigorous questions, I gave myself very few expert-level ratings initially. But there are always improvements to be made. If you find yourself scoring a lot of 5s, you might need to reflect in more depth.

Don't forget that you are rating your questioning behavior. This involves more than just the questions you ask. It also involves the environment you set for your students. Do you create a culture in which asking rigorous questions is simply expected in class, not just from the teacher, but from the students as well? This behavior rating scale asks you to look at your questioning skills on more than a superficial level. This rating scales asks you to consider if effective questioning behavior is in the very DNA of your classroom.

HOW DO YOU RATE YOUR QUESTIONING BEHAVIOR?

1. How often do you challenge students by asking questions that arouse their curiosity or make them want to know more?

   1   2   3   4   5

2. Do your questions encourage students to listen to each other's responses and opinions?

   1   2   3   4   5

3. Do your questions promote self-evaluation by your students?

   1   2   3   4   5

4. Do you preplan key questions you want to ask during the lesson?

   1   2   3   4   5

5. Do your questions call for students to think for themselves?

   1   2   3   4   5

6. Do you ask a variety of questions—recall versus thoughtful questions?

   1   2   3   4   5

7. Do all students get involved in class discussions?

   1   2   3   4   5

8. Do students speak to each other when responding or only to you?

   1   2   3   4   5

9. Do you wait a reasonable time for students to think about their responses before calling on them or permitting them to speak?

   1   2   3   4   5

10. Do you encourage your students to ask questions?

    1   2   3   4   5

	Now add up your score and use the following scale to rate your questioning behavior:
45–50	Your questioning behavior is off the charts, literally. Students are being pushed to reach their potential through your questions and theirs.
39–44	Your questioning behavior is above average and needs minimal refining.
33–38	Your questioning behavior is pretty good but could use some consistency.
27–32	Your questioning behavior shows that you need to put more work into the types of questions you ask and the classroom culture you create for your students.
21–26	You might want to take a good look at the questions you ask in class and what they are designed to do.
0–20	Your questioning behavior needs a major overhaul, but the good news is that this book is designed to provide you will the skills to do so.

ABOUT THIS BOOK

The first chapter provides a rationale for using higher level questioning in order to promote rigor in the classroom. What is the research behind higher level questioning, and how do you know that higher level questioning will be effective with your students? Chapter 2 distinguishes the difference between difficulty and rigor. Having a good understanding of the difference is important because some educators think of them as the same concept, but they are not. Chapters 3–6 scaffold your understanding of higher level questioning and provide guidance through activities and exemplars, showing you how to generate your own questions and take existing lower level questions and transform them into rigorous, higher level questions.

Then, you will apply what you have learned about higher level questions to your own written assessments in Chapter 7. Beyond that, Chapter 8 provides tips and guidance for asking questions in class and developing techniques that allow you to generate effective questions on the go. Of course, effective questioning is about more than just writing and asking questions. It is about creating an environment in which higher level thinking is simply the norm. Chapter 9 shows you how to develop a rigorous classroom so that higher level questions are just an everyday part of class, including strategies for empowering students to ask higher level questions of their own.

Each chapter begins with an essential question to get you thinking about the chapter's focus. The end of each chapter features a series of questions meant to help you process and reflect on what was covered. Take some time and put thought into your responses. You do not have to write your responses down; however, by doing so, you will create a valuable record of your thoughts at the time of reading that could be revisited later.

By the end of this book, you will have the tools in order to practice promoting rigor in your classroom, on your classroom assignments, and with your students. Your classroom will be growing into a higher level thinking environment, and your students will be better learners. Your willingness to try the strategies from this book in your classroom and do what is best for students will benefit many. For that, I thank you.

REFLECTION QUESTIONS

1. Were you surprised at your questioning behavior rating, or do you think it provides a clear picture of the type of questioner you are?

2. How do you think your students would rate your questioning behavior?
3. Do you feel your school has a culture of challenging students to think at higher levels?
4. Try to remember a teacher you had in school or a past/current colleague who asked really good questions. How would you describe his or her classroom culture?
5. Are you willing to be open-minded and try strategies that are out of your comfort zone during the course of this book?

Chapter 1

Getting Started With Higher Level Questioning

Essential Question
How can you use higher level questioning to make your classroom more rigorous?

Socrates is considered by many to be one of the greatest thinkers in history. He wrestled with philosophical topics such as morality, virtue, knowledge, and politics. He is well-known for the Socratic method, a form of cooperative dialogue that is based on asking questions until participants arrive at the truth. In order to arrive at the truth, you have to ask the right questions, building upon the answers to formulate additional questions. This is what it looks like if I were having a conversation with my youngest daughter:

My daughter:	"I just love dogs."
Me:	"What is it about dogs that you love so much?"
My daughter:	"They're so cute."
Me:	"What, specifically, is so cute about them?"
My daughter:	"They're so soft."
Me:	"So you like the soft coat of a dog. What about dogs with coarser coats, such as a poodle or a bulldog?"
My daughter:	"No, I love them, too."
Me:	"Maybe it's not their softness that makes you love dogs so much. Maybe it's something else?"
My daughter:	"I suppose it could be."
Me:	"What is the first thing you notice when you see a dog?"
My daughter:	"Its tongue."
Me:	"What about its tongue?"
My daughter:	"How it hangs out of its mouth like it's smiling."
Me:	"So you like dogs' tongues?"
My daughter:	"I like when they lick me with them. It shows me they love me."
Me:	"Are you saying that what you enjoy is that dogs show love so much?"
My daughter:	"Yes, that is what I love about dogs."

This conversation took a little while, but with some persistent questioning, we arrived at a much deeper response than simply that my daughter loves dogs. In the examination, she discovered why she loves dogs so much. At first she thought it was their softness, but with further questioning, she realized that was not accurate. She really just loves that dogs are extremely loving, and she was able to associate that with their tongues.

This method can be used with much weightier issues. Take this conversation, for instance, between a mother and son:

Son:	"I'm afraid of death."
Mother:	"What about death is so frightening?"
Son:	"That you're no longer here, that you're somewhere else."
Mother:	"And you don't think that somewhere else is going to be a good place?"
Son:	"I would like to hope it is."
Mother:	"But you're not sure?"
Son:	"No, I'm not sure."
Mother:	"What if you knew that it was a good place?"
Son:	"Then it probably wouldn't seem so bad."
Mother:	"And you wouldn't be as afraid?"
Son:	"Probably not."
Mother:	"What I'm hearing you say is that you aren't afraid of actual death; you're afraid because you don't know what happens after death. Is that correct?
Son:	"Yes, I suppose that is."
Mother:	"So your fear is more about the unknown?"
Son:	"Yes, that is my fear."

This conversation involves a much heftier topic than the conversation I had with my daughter, but the takeaway is similar. Someone states something, and through a series of questions designed to explore the topic further, you arrive at something much deeper. You understand not only the "what," but also, more importantly, the "why."

This type of questioning can be applied to more than philosophical issues. Consider this conversation in an elementary math classroom, in which a student has not yet learned subtraction:

Student:	"The answer is 14."
Teacher:	"And how did you arrive at that answer?"
Student:	"I don't know."

Teacher: "But you do know because you got the answer correct. How did you do that?"

Student: "I added the two numbers, 8 and 6, together, and they equal 14."

Teacher: "How did you know to add the numbers?"

Student: "There was the plus sign between the numbers."

Teacher: "What if there had been a minus sign in its place?"

Student: "Then I would have gotten a different answer."

Teacher: "Why is that?"

Student: "Because in addition you add the numbers together, and when there is a minus you subtract one from the other."

Teacher: "Why does that make the answers different?"

Student: "Because in addition the answer is always greater than the numbers used in the problem."

Teacher: "And how is this different with subtraction? Is the number not bigger when you subtract?"

Student: "No."

Teacher: "What is it?"

Student: "It's smaller."

Teacher: "Why does it become smaller?"

Student: "Because you are taking one number away from the other."

Teacher: "Which makes it smaller?"

Student: "Yes."

Teacher: "What would the smaller number be if the problem was 8 − 6?"

Student: "I don't know."

Teacher: "But you do. You said you take the number away from the other. When you take 6 away from 8, what is left?"

Student: "2."

Teacher: "Great. Is it smaller than both numbers?"

Student: "Yes."

Teacher:	"Does it always have to be smaller than both of the numbers?"
Student:	"I think so."
Teacher:	"What if we took 8 and subtracted 2? What would be left?"
Student:	"6."
Teacher:	"Is that smaller than both numbers?"
Student:	"No, just the first one."
Teacher:	"So we can assume that in subtraction, the answer is always smaller than the first number."
Student:	"We can."

Simply by answering some follow-up questions, this student is learning the basic concepts of subtraction, using his prior knowledge of addition to grasp a new concept. These conversations all display the power of higher level questions.

THE BENEFITS OF USING HIGHER LEVEL QUESTIONS IN YOUR CLASSROOM

Are there benefits to using higher level questions with your students? You might think that this question involves an obvious answer. Of course, there are many benefits to using higher level questions in your classroom, but I want to present some of the reasoning behind the importance of higher level questions and thinking. Using higher level questions in your classroom:

» improves student achievement,
» builds understanding and retention of learning,
» increases student engagement,
» asks students to think for themselves, and
» teaches valuable 21st-century skills.

IMPROVE STUDENT ACHIEVEMENT

When considering student achievement, the groundbreaking work of Hattie (2018) is a great place to start. Throughout his career, he has looked at many practices and research and determined which factors have the greatest effect on student achievement. Figure 2 shows some of the results for purposes of this discussion (you can see the complete list at https://visible-learning.org/hattie-ranking-influences-effect-sizes-learning-achievement). An effect size above .4 means a factor is effective; anything below that is ineffective. Note that Hattie does not explicitly use the exact phrasing "higher level questioning" as one of the strategies. You will notice that "questioning" is only rated a .48, but the other related factors listed in Figure 2 all employ higher thinking skills. This shows that questioning by itself is mildly effective, but when you ask students the right questions that require them to think at a higher level, such as through cognitive task analysis, evaluation, and creativity, the effect on achievement is much stronger. When you also consider that classroom discussion, a strategy that employs higher level questions, rates at a .82, it becomes even clearer that higher level questions designed to allow students to think are, indeed, an effective practice for improving student achievement.

BUILD UNDERSTANDING AND RETENTION

Higher level questioning helps students gain understanding. If you ask lower level questions, you essentially require them to access the part of their brain that has memorized a term or concept and to duplicate it in the form of an answer. Knowing something and understanding something are completely different. Knowing a concept does not mean students can create with it, adapt it to apply to another concept, or break it down and look at its various components. These are all acts of thinking.

For example, when learning about airplane flight, you might come across the following information:

Factor	Effect Size
Cognitive task analysis	1.29
Classroom discussion	.82
Evaluation and reflection	.75
Problem solving teaching	.68
Creativity programs	.62
Meta-cognitive strategies	.60
Questioning	.48

FIGURE 2. Hattie's (2018) factors related to student achievement that involve higher level thinking.

When air rushes over the curved upper wing surface, it has to travel further than the air that passes underneath, so it has to go faster (to cover more distance in the same time). According to a principle of aerodynamics called Bernoulli's law, fast-moving air is at lower pressure than slow-moving air, so the pressure above the wing is lower than the pressure below, and this creates the lift that powers the plane upward. (Woodford, 2019, para. 7)

A student might read this information or watch a video on the principles of flight. When the student is asked "How are airplanes able to fly?", he could recite this definition and be correct. That does not mean that the student understands how flying works. The student may not be able to explain how the lift on a stunt plane flying upside now does not have the opposite effect and instantly send the plane downward. If, however, a student has an understanding of how lift works, he would be able to determine possible solutions to this dilemma.

If the teacher asked, "How are paper airplanes able to fly even though they typically have flat wings that would not be able to produce lift?", a student who only "knows" the definition would have difficulty making sense of this. The student who understands it might be able to discern that:

paper airplanes are really gliders, converting altitude to forward motion. Lift comes when the air below the airplane wing is pushing up harder than the air above it is pushing down. It is this difference in pressure that enables the plane to fly. Pressure can be reduced on a wing's surface by making the air move over it more quickly. The wings of a plane are curved so that the air moves more quickly over the top of the wing, resulting in an upward push, or lift, on the wing. (Scholastic, n.d. para. 3)

Why is understanding so important? If students know the answers, isn't knowledge enough? Understanding leads to better retention. As a teacher, preparing a lesson for students over days or weeks, only to find a month down the road that the students do not really remember the information well enough to use it, can be extremely frustrating. This can be especially devastating in math and English language arts (ELA), where you expect students to build upon a foundation of knowledge. If the foundation is not solid, the rest of students' learning will suffer. According to Cardellichio and Field (1997), higher order questions increase neural branching, which means students are going to retain what they are learning. The process of neural branching can be promoted through seven types of questions:

1. **Hypothetical thinking:** This form of thinking is used to create new information. It asks students to develop answers based on generalizations related to the posed situation. These questions follow general forms, such as "What if [this] happened?" or "What if [this] were not true?"

2. **Reversal thinking:** This type of thinking requires students to turn a question around and look for opposite ideas. For example: "What happens if I reverse the addends in a math problem?" "What caused this?" "How does it change if I go backward?"

3. **Application of different symbol systems:** This way of thinking is to apply a symbol system to a situation for

which it is not usually used, such as writing a math equation to show how animal interaction is related.

4. **Analogy:** This process of thinking asks students to compare unrelated situations, such as how the Pythagorean theorem is related to cooking. For example: "How is ___ like ___?"

5. **Analysis of point of view:** This way of thinking requires students to consider and question other people's perspectives, beliefs, or opinions in order to extend their minds. For instance, a teacher may ask a student, "What else could account for this?" or "How many other ways could someone look at this?"

6. **Completion:** This form of thinking requires students to finish an incomplete project or situation that would normally be completed, such as removing the end of a story and expecting students to create their own ending.

7. **Web analysis:** With web analysis, students must synthesize how events are related in complex ways instead of simply relying on the brain's natural ability to develop a simple pattern. For example: "How extensive were the effects of ___?" or "Track the relationship of events following from ___."

All of these types of questions fall under the higher level order and are designed to help students better retain what they have learned by understanding it.

INCREASE STUDENT ENGAGEMENT

The third benefit to higher level questioning is that it just makes for a livelier classroom. Consider the following two classrooms and their questioning practices.

Classroom 1:

Teacher: Who can tell me what an ecosystem is?

Student 1:   Where animals and plants live in one area.

Teacher: Can someone give me an example of an
                    ecosystem?
Student 2:   A desert.
Teacher: Can someone give me another example?
Student 3:   The ocean.
Teacher: What are the producers in both of these
                    ecosystems?
Student 4:   Plants.
Teacher: What ecosystem might you find a bear in?
Student 5:   A forest.

Classroom 2:
Teacher: Who can tell me what an ecosystem is?
Student 1:   Where animals and plants live in one area.
Teacher: Do both plants and animals need to be there?
Student 2:   I think so.
Teacher: What would happen if you didn't have one of
                    them?
Student 3:   The ecosystem would probably die.
Teacher: Why would that happen?
Student 4:   Because they depend on one another. The
                    animals eat the plants, and then other ani-
                    mals eat those animals. Without plants those
                    animals would die out, and then the other
                    animals' food source would be gone as well,
                    and they would die out.
Teacher: Which ecosystem do you think would be bet-
                    ter to live in, the desert or the ocean?
Student 5:   I would say the ocean because food in the
                    desert would be scarce. Your chances of find-
                    ing food in the ocean are far greater given the
                    abundance of sea life.

Which classroom seems more interesting? One indicator
would be the length of the answers. In Classroom 1, notice that
the answers are all short and do not require the students to expand
on them. This isn't because those students are less interested or do

not know as much. It is because the questions only required one- or two-word answers. One thing I have learned about students is that they will give you what you ask for—no more, no less. If you ask questions that elicit short responses, that is what you are going to get. That is why your questions need to give students some room to explore and explain. Classroom 2 started out with the same first question, but then the teacher began to ask questions that could not be answered in one or two words. The answers needed to be explained. This makes for a more engaging classroom, and if higher level questioning becomes part of your classroom culture, students will anticipate that they will need to give more detailed answers, keeping them engaged and more on their toes.

Why is student engagement so important? A study by the Gallup Poll shows that the longer students are in school, the less engaged them become (Busteed, 2013):

> The Gallup Student Poll surveyed nearly 500,000 students in grades five through 12 from more than 1,700 public schools in 37 states in 2012. We found that nearly eight in 10 elementary students who participated in the poll are engaged with school. By middle school that falls to about six in 10 students. And by high school, only four in 10 students qualify as engaged. (para. 3)

As noted, by the time students reach high school where they should be learning about more thoughtful and deeper topics, they are less engaged. This lack of engagement can lead to disillusionment with school and can cause many students to underachieve due to lack of motivation. According to Smart and Marshall (2012), teacher questioning has been identified as a critical factor in facilitating effective discourse in the classroom, especially in the area of supporting students' engagement. Imagine if educators could keep high school students engaged with teaching techniques such as higher level questioning. This would allow students to care more about school and, as a result, learn more.

ASK STUDENTS TO THINK FOR THEMSELVES

Higher level questioning requires students to think for themselves. Students often play a passive role in the classroom, receiving information from the teacher in a basic lecture format. They do not engage in thinking for themselves; thus, they have difficulty problem solving or using critical thinking skills. This ability to critically think is so important, not just in academics, but in life. In a study on predicting real-world outcomes, Butler, Pentoney, and Bong (2017) came to the conclusion that critical thinking skills are a much better indicator of a person's ability to make positive life decisions than a person's raw intelligence:

> Over one hundred years of research on intelligence testing has shown that scores on standardized tests of intelligence predict a wide range of outcomes, but even the strongest advocates of intelligence testing agree that IQ scores . . . leave a large portion of the variance unexplained when predicting real-life behaviors . . . critical thinking ability had a greater association with real life decisions, and it added significantly to explained variance, beyond what was accounted for by intelligence alone. (p. 44)

Cox (n.d.) talked about 10 strategies that enhance student thinking. Amongst these are:

» building a classroom in which students feel that they can ask questions without any negative reactions from their peers or teachers, and in which students feel free to be creative;

» promoting higher order thinking that requires students to really understand a concept, not repeat it or memorize it;

» utilizing Question-Answer-Relationships, or QARs, that teach students to label the type of question that is being asked and then use that information to help them formulate an answer;

» teaching students to make inferences by giving them real-world examples; and

» teaching students to use a step-by-step method for solving problems.

All of these strategies can be accomplished by asking students the right types of questions. Ultimately, students should be in an environment in which they learn to question for themselves through self-questioning.

TEACH 21ST-CENTURY SKILLS

The fifth benefit of higher level thinking is its ability to enhance 21st-century skills. The Partnership for 21st Century Skills (2011) championed the 4 C's:
» creativity,
» collaboration,
» communication, and
» critical thinking.

Each of these skills can be nurtured through higher level questioning.

In order to foster creativity, you have to foster curiosity. You might accomplish this by asking students to make meaningful connections between their interests and what they are learning in class. You also have to build opportunities for collaboration through classroom discussions. If you build an effective discussion (see Chapter 8), students feed off each other's knowledge in a collaborative thinking environment. One student's responses might spark a passion for a concept in another student or build another student's understanding. Students learn together through higher level questioning and become better collaborators by listening to and respecting others' ideas.

When it comes to communication, being able to ask proper, thought-provoking questions is an effective way to target and gather information. Students can learn to pose follow-up questions when they do not understand a topic. Communication becomes the key to filling gaps in students' understanding of concepts. Lastly, questions can be used to challenge a student's assumptions and lead to critical thinking. Students who are exposed to better questions are able to recognize the importance of questioning in the problem-solving process. The higher level a question, the more in-depth thinking will take place, meaning that multiple solutions might be discovered as possible answers to a problem.

Why are these 21st-century skills important? There is a direct link between the development of 21st-century skills and quality work. According to one study, young adults who experienced high 21st-century skill development in school self-reported high work quality in the workplace (17%) at twice the rate as those with medium (8%) and low development (8%; Levy & Sidhu, 2013). Unfortunately, most of the 1,014 respondents in the study did not experience 21st-century skill development while in school. The researchers concluded that a majority of respondents (59%) learned 21st-century skills while on the job, not from school. The researchers found that schools could significantly impact students' long-term work success by purposely teaching more 21st-century skills. This is why using higher level questioning and getting students to think more will equip students for not just the present, but the future as well.

WHY DOESN'T EVERYONE USE HIGHER LEVEL THINKING IN THE CLASSROOM?

Higher order thinking questions are not being utilized in the classroom as effectively and as often as possible. McRel International collected classroom observation data and found that only approximately one out of every four questions teachers ask in the classroom is higher level, as defined by Bloom's (1956) taxonomy (Abla & Maxfield, 2017). That means three out of every four questions are not. This goes back to that questioning behavior you considered in the introduction. How do you rate these teachers' questioning behavior based on the data?

Why aren't all teachers using higher level questioning in the classroom? One reason could be that many teachers have an easier time using lower level questions, especially when creating assessments that are easier to grade. A larger issue, however, is awareness. Many teachers are not even aware that they are not asking many higher level questions. Because they are unaware, they do not think there is something that needs to be improved. That's where this book and your growing understanding come in.

REFLECTION QUESTIONS

1. Review the five advantages of higher level questioning discussed in this chapter. Which do you feel is most important for your students to possess, and why?

2. How confident do you feel that your students understand what you are teaching, rather than them just "knowing" the content? What can you do to improve students' understanding?

3. Consider the five advantages of higher level questioning. Which do you feel you need to work on most in your own classroom? Why?

4. When you think about the teaching strategies you have employed in your classroom, which one(s) got the students more engaged? Why do you suppose this is the case?

5. Do you need more convincing as to the benefit of higher level questioning in your classroom, or do you agree its advantages far outweigh the additional work it will take you to use this strategy consistently in your classroom? Why or why not?

Chapter 2

The Difference Between Difficulty and Rigor

Changing Your Mindset

Essential Question

How do you distinguish between a question that is difficult and a question that is rigorous?

Many educators do not know what *rigor* actually means. They equate creating a more rigorous classroom with developing a more difficult classroom. And how do they make class harder? The easiest way is by giving students more things to do and less time to do them. This, my friend, is not rigor. In fact, many students resent just being given more, especially if it involves more of the same work. Rigor requires providing different work that is going to challenge students. The best way to challenge students is by challenging their thinking—by asking them the right questions.

Perhaps the biggest misconception for educators when developing questions is the belief that if a question is hard or difficult, then it is rigorous. The perfect example of this is the game show *Jeopardy!* in which contestants are presented with an answer and they must respond with the correct question. For example, a contestant might be provided with the following answer:

> This person won the Oscar for screenwriting an original script at the 1977 Academy Awards.

The correct response is pretty difficult to figure out. You would need to have a substantial knowledge of Academy Award history or a memory of watching the award show that year. To come up with a response, you could not use reasoning or critical thinking. The answer is out there—you just might not have it. This *Jeopardy!* challenge is difficult, but is it rigorous? The Glossary of Education Reform (Great Schools Partnership, 2014) defined rigor in the following way:

> In education, *rigor* is commonly applied to lessons that encourage students to question their assumptions and think deeply, rather than to lessons that merely demand memorization and information recall. (para. 2)

Notice the phrase *think deeply*. Rigorous questions require thinking—not just any thinking. They require higher levels of thinking.

To respond to the *Jeopardy!* example, one must possess knowledge, but is the mere possession of knowledge a higher order thinking skill? Actually, knowledge usually comes down to rote memorization, one of the most basic forms of thinking. The *Jeopardy!* example involves accessing your stored knowledge. Sometimes you are successful and you access the answer, and sometimes you do not, but no higher order thinking takes place. You are not weighing options or pondering a problem that could involve multiple solutions. You have been asked a close-ended question with one correct answer.

Unfortunately, this is how a lot of learning in school is set up. Teachers provide students with information, either directly or indirectly, and then students are simply asked to recall the information. There are times when teachers try to make it a bit more challenging by having students apply what they learned to come up with a different answer than what they were told, but students are still evaluated on whether they displayed or applied the knowledge correctly or not.

A simple example of this would be the skill of addition. Students are not provided with every possible problem that could be formulated and then given all of the possible answers for each of these problems. Students are taught addition so that they can apply it to any numbers they want to. As students become more proficient, they can add larger numbers and multiple sets, but they are still using the simple skill of addition. They are merely accessing that skill and then applying it to the situation.

CAN YOU TELL THE DIFFERENCE?

Rather than just theorizing whether you know the difference between difficulty and rigor, let us put it into practice. The following are 10 questions that might be asked in a classroom. Determine whether you think the question is a difficult (D) or rigorous (R).

1. What is the circumference of the Earth?	D	R
2. When should you use the Pythagorean theorem?	D	R
3. What is the best form of government?	D	R
4. Why is the sky blue?	D	R
5. What is the theme of the book?	D	R
6. Did you like the movie?	D	R

7. Why do you think the Germans decided to fight a two-front war during World War II?	D	R
8. How do you change a tire?	D	R
9. What is a good reason for picking a certain computer?	D	R
10. Why do you think tennis is scored the way it is?	D	R

Now let us take a look at each of these and the reasoning as to why they are difficult or rigorous:

1. *What is the circumference of the Earth?* Difficult. This question might be challenging because the concept is not something that students encounter on a daily basis. However, this is not a rigorous question because scientists have determined the precise circumference of the Earth, meaning students could look up the answer.

2. *When should you use the Pythagorean theorem?* Difficult. The Pythagorean theorem can be quite complex, and it can be difficult to determine how to apply it. However, there are clear situations in which applying the theorem is correct.

3. *What is the best form of government?* Rigorous. No authority has determined which form of government is the best. Different countries choose different governments for different reasons that make sense to them. Students would have to justify their answers.

4. *Why is the sky blue?* Difficult or Rigorous. This question could be either depending upon the intent of the question. If you are in science class and you ask students this question, there is a definitive answer as to what makes the sky blue. However, if you are asking a group of younger students why they think the sky is blue, they could come up with all sorts of creative and imaginative responses, ranging from that it has to be blue because the yellow from the sun and the blue in the sky make the grass green, to that's the crayon that was pulled from the box when creating the sky.

5. *What is the theme of the book?* Difficult. The theme is probably not going to be explicitly stated in the book, but there will be numerous concrete clues that point a student in the right direction. The theme might have to be inferred, but it is still based off of content knowledge.

6. *Did you like the movie?* Rigorous. Although a movie might be popular, others may not have enjoyed it. Students would have to justify their answers.

7. *Why do you think the Germans decided to fight a two-front war during World War II?* Rigorous. Although there is a lot of speculation as to why Germany did this, with many experts weighing in, there is no document showing the sole reason Germany decided to fight against the Allies to the west and Russia to the east and divide its army. Students could use reasoning to develop their own theory as to why the Germans did this.

8. *How do you change a tire?* Difficult. Not everyone knows how to change a tire, and it can be a challenge to do so, but there is a proper way.

9. *What is a good reason for picking a certain computer?* Rigorous. Different people are going to have different reasons for choosing a particular computer. Students would have to justify their answers.

10. *Why do you think tennis is scored the way it is?* Rigorous. This question does not have a definitive answer. Followers of the sport are not quite sure how the system of love, 15, 30, and 40 was developed. There are all sorts of theories, but nothing is known for sure.

DEVELOPING RIGOROUS TASKS AND ASSESSMENTS

The importance of knowing the difference between difficulty and rigor carries over into student tasks and assessments. How do you develop rigorous student activities and assessments? You start with asking more difficult questions, but again, this alone does not build rigor. For example, on an end-of-unit assessment, you could ask students to provide the atomic weight of oxygen. The answer (~16 amu) might not be common knowledge, but it is a recorded fact. Therein lies the problem. Just like giving students more of the same work, asking only knowledge-based questions will not challenge students' thinking.

To provide an example of different types of thinking, a teacher could ask this open-ended question: "What is your favorite book, and why?" Students will not have to struggle to determine their favorite book (although some might have a hard time choosing). They will, however, need to consider their "why." Often, students know that they like something, but they cannot point to what exactly they like about it. But asking students what elements of the book they enjoyed will require them to access a higher level of thinking. They may have to *think deeply* to justify their "why."

The question becomes: How much higher order thinking is being asked of your students in the classroom? I do not just mean the large assignments that address essential questions; I mean in their day-to-day experiences in the class. How much higher level thinking is being asked of students on a pencil-and-paper test? How much higher level thinking is involved in the questions you ask or propose in a discussion? How much higher level thinking is displayed in the daily work students produce to show mastery?

Should every activity or lesson involve only higher level thinking? Absolutely not. The lower levels of thinking have their place in the classroom. They act as the building blocks to higher thinking. Without basic knowledge, students cannot begin to think critically. Problems develop when teachers stop at the lower level rather than pushing students into the higher range.

SELF-ASSESSING YOUR CLASSROOM'S HIGHER LEVEL THINKING RATIO

The ratio of higher to lower level thinking that students do in class should be about 50:50. How do you determine whether or not you are achieving this ratio? Look at your artifacts—anything you give to students, whether it be a worksheet, an assessment, or a homework assignment. Look at the posters you have up in your classroom or the questions you ask students at the start of class. Analyze these artifacts to determine your ratio of higher to lower level thinking. If you are asking most of your questions in the lower level sections, you need to determine whether or not this indicates that your class lacks rigor. If, through this self-assessment, you think your classroom displays a lack of rigor, you might need to revise and edit the work you ask your students to complete. Build in more higher level thinking and rigor.

Teachers do a lot of prep work, from creating projects and activities, to developing assignments or other strategies to teach their students. There are also the day-to-day questions you ask students. If most of the questions you ask of your class have a definitive correct answer, you are probably asking too many lower level questions. If, however, students have several different ways that they could answer a question, they are having to think critically and access more higher level thinking skills.

MAKING DIFFICULT QUESTIONS MORE RIGOROUS

Your ratio of higher level to lower level questions can sometimes be easily balanced with just a little creative wordsmithing. You can take a difficult question and make it rigorous or simply add a follow-up question that takes the initial question into rigorous territory.

Let us use the examples of difficult questions we looked at earlier:

» What is the circumference of the Earth?
» When should you use the Pythagorean theory?
» Why is the sky blue?
» What is the theme of the book?
» How do you change a tire?

With a few adjustments, you can make a difficult question rigorous:

» *What is the circumference of Krypton?* Because this is a fictitious planet, no one really knows the answer. You could certainly take the description of the planet from the comics and speculate, as well as use information from what we know about the Earth's circumference.

» *When should you use the Pythagorean theorem? What would happen if what you were measuring did not have a right angle in it?* Typically, the Pythagorean theorem can only be applied to a triangle containing a right angle. Students would have to discern whether the formula could even be applied without one.

» *Why is the sky blue? What color would it be to fish?* Because fish live underwater, and their vision is filtered through the water, do they see the sky as anything other than blue? We can certainly make a hypothesis based on what we do know about fish, but we do not have photos or proof, nor can we interview a fish to find out.

» *What is the theme of the book* Frankenstein? *What if the story had been told from the point of view of the monster? How would that change the theme?* The theme of the book changes mightily if told from the monster's point of view. Instead of being about Victor's ambition, the focus would shift to determining how to be human.

» *How do you change a tire without a jack?* There is certainly a correct way to change a tire when you have a jack, but what would you have to do if you didn't have one? There could be all sorts of creative ways to try to accomplish this feat.

Notice that, in most of the revised questions, students would still have to have a basic understanding of the concept or skill in order to apply it in a new way. The new questions, however, take each concept to a new level of thinking by asking students to think critically.

Reflecting on the level of thinking your work requires of students can result in some changes to your classroom. Hopefully, some of these changes develop more higher order thinking in your classroom, which can immediately increase the rigor of your classroom. This is certainly going to take some ongoing work, not only in developing higher level questions ahead of time, but also in training yourself so that you can ask higher level questions on the go. Keep in mind that raising the rigor in your classroom means raising the rigor of your teaching, but just as your students will be better learners, you will be a better teacher.

REFLECTION QUESTIONS

1. What do you think is the ratio of higher to lower level questions used in your classroom? Are you satisfied with the answer?

2. How adept were you at determining which questions were rigorous questions and which ones were difficult in the "Can You Tell the Difference?" section in this chapter? Are you as skilled at this when looking at your own questions? How could you improve?

3. Do you think you use rigorous questions consistently in your classroom, from assessments to assignments, to activities to discussions? Which one of these areas do you think needs the most improvement? Why?

4. Do you feel that curriculum, common/state assessments, and/or resources provided assist or impede your ability to ask higher level questions? Why?

5. How willing are you to make changes in your questions in order to make them more rigorous and challenging for students?

Chapter 3

Building
Question
Awareness

Essential Question
Do you have a system that helps you
determine the difference between a
higher and a lower level question?

In order to successfully evaluate your questioning rating, you have to be able to tell the difference between levels of thinking used in the questions. Part of building your own question awareness (i.e., recognizing the types or levels of questions you are asking) comes in being able to categorize your questions. If you are using a clear system in order to determine the rigor of each question you ask, then you will better understand whether you are asking enough higher level questions. Trying to guess your ratio of higher to lower level questions can result in an inaccurate assessment of your questioning abilities. Being able to gather and analyze accurate data about your questioning practices will help you gain a clearer picture of your classroom environment.

Using an established question system can be helpful when it comes to categorizing your questioning abilities. Following a structure allows you to more clearly identify the types of questions you are asking, making you more aware of when you are relying too heavily on lower level questions. After all, if you are not able to identify what type of question you are asking, how can you possibly reflect upon your questioning techniques? There are various systems for developing questions. You need to use one (or a combination) that works best for you.

Five questioning systems are discussed in this chapter:

- » the five Ws,
- » convergent versus divergent questions,
- » Costa's three levels of questioning,
- » Webb's depth of knowledge, and
- » Fusco's questioning strategies.

THE FIVE Ws

One of the more basic systems of questioning is the reliable five Ws (and one H). These question stems—Who? What? When? Where? Why? How?—form the basis for most questions. In most cases, the five Ws are divided into lower and higher level (see Figure 3).

For instance, if your language arts class is reading the book *And Then There Were None* by Agatha Christie, you could form a series of questions based on these question stems:

- » Who is the first person killed in the book?
- » What is the reason all of these people have been targeted for death?

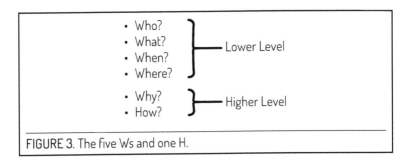

FIGURE 3. The five Ws and one H.

» When does this book take place?

» Where is the book's setting?

» Why do you agree or disagree that the people on this island deserved to die?

» How do you think characters could have behaved differently to avoid their fate?

The who, what, when, and where questions in this example can all be answered if someone has read the book because the author has provided all of the information. The why and how questions, however, ask for answers beyond the scope of the book. They ask students to state an opinion and justify it, as well as wonder how the story might have changed had something been different. Students might use context and logic from the book to arrive at their answers, but each student's answers will likely differ from other students', while still being correct.

The five Ws are a simple way to get started with higher and lower level questions. Also, especially if you are teaching lower grades, the five Ws will help the students better their questioning practices. The who, what, when, and where questions require facts in order to be answered; thus, they generally generate close-ended questions with definitive answers. The why and the how tend to access deeper thinking because they push students to think beyond recall of facts. They cause students to pause and ponder more about the answer. How and why questions also work as effective follow-up questions to push lower level questions to a higher level.

For example, "What is your favorite season?" requires students to know the four seasons and then determine their favorite based on the typical characteristics of these seasons (e.g., summer is hot, winter is cold, spring is rainy, fall is moderate, etc.). Note, however, that this question only requires a one-word answer from students. But if you follow this question with a simple "Why is it your favorite season?" then students have to dig a little deeper and justify their choice. They may access personal memories that make them feel a certain way about a season. This follow-up question requires students to not only state what their favorite season is, but also consider why someone else should like it. This justification involves using higher order thinking in order to make an argument.

The five Ws can lead to problems because, as discussed here, using these question stems does not guarantee that a question involves higher level thinking. Utilizing why or how in a question does not necessarily mean the question is higher level. Consider the previous examples from *And Then There Were None*. Those questions could have been:

» Why do the few remaining survivors believe they are alone on the island?

» How does Wargrave die?

Both of these new examples are recall questions, requiring students to use information they read in the book. At the same time, the lower thinking stems could be adapted into higher level questions:

» What do you think you would have done if you were stranded on the island?

» Who did you think the killer was before the reveal, and what led you to this conclusion?

» Is where this story takes place important to the plot, or could the story have been set anywhere?

» Is when this story takes place necessary, or could the story be set in modern times?

Like any of the systems shared in this chapter, the stems that are used do not guarantee the level of the question. When using the five Ws, you have to pay close attention to whether questions are higher or lower level.

CONVERGENT VERSUS DIVERGENT QUESTIONS

Questions can be categorized as convergent or divergent. The difference comes down to whether the question is close-ended or open-ended. A convergent question has a defined correct answer. The answer is recalled from information that was either read or encountered, but is typically not the student's own creation. Convergent thinking means bringing together facts and converging them into a single, usually concise, answer (see Figure 4).

Convergent questions are designed to try to help one find a solution to a problem. Examples of convergent questions might include:

» What was the major cause of World War I?
» How does a hummingbird fly?
» Why should you not end a sentence with a preposition?
» What does 15 divided by 3 equal?
» Where is the Louvre located?

All of these examples can be answered with short statements, no more than a sentence or two, but there are convergent questions that could require longer answers. This does not make them deeper thinking questions, however. They still involve recall, but students may just need to recall a lot more information in order to answer them correctly.

A divergent question is usually more open-ended. It adds layers to a convergent response because students still need to recall some information, but they need to add to that information by analyzing, judging, or creating, and consider multiple solutions (see Figure 5). Because there are several potential answers, stu-

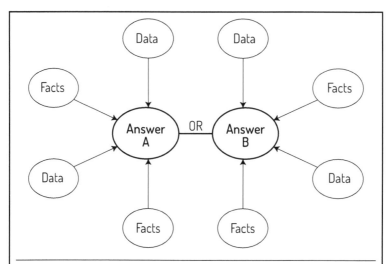

FIGURE 4. Convergent thinking. From "A Map of How Convergent Thinking Works," by Msingh209, 2012, retrieved from https://en.wikipedia.org/wiki/Convergent_thinking#/media/File:Map_of_Convergent_Thinking.jpg. CC BY-SA 3.0.

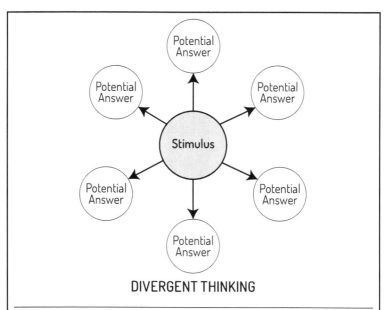

DIVERGENT THINKING

FIGURE 5. Divergent thinking. From "A Map of How Divergent Thinking Works," by Aishwarya.gudadhe, 2015, retrieved from https://en.wikipedia.org/wiki/Divergent_thinking#/media/File:Final_divergent_thinking.jpg. CC BY-SA 4.0.

dents have to weigh the possibilities and determine which one would be the best answer based on whatever criterion they need to or have decided to use—whether it be the answer that is the most creative, the most logical, or the most efficient. This criterion might be explicit or implicit.

For example, consider the question, "What is the best movie ever?" If you ask 30 different people, you are likely to get 30 different answers, all based on respondents' personal criterion. Someone might be into comedies; thus his list is headlined by *Caddyshack*. Another person might be a musical fan; thus *West Side Story* is his pick. A different musical lover might say that *La La Land* is her choice. There is no wrong answer. That is the challenge of divergent questions—almost any answer could be justified. That can make divergent questions difficult to assess.

Examples of divergent questions might include:

» What was the most important invention of the 20th century?

» Why do geese walk across the road when they could fly?

» Why is it important that we write well?

» What are 10 different equations that could produce an answer of 15?

» Is art necessary?

You can see the clear difference between a convergent and divergent question. In most cases, you are looking for whether a question has a clear, definitive answer that requires logic (convergent) or whether there is room for many possible answers that require imagination (divergent).

Of course, we know that sometimes things are not so black and white. Sometimes questions can fall into both categories. That is why convergent and divergent can be categorized further to help to identify these differences (Gallagher & Aschner, 1963):

» **Level I: Low Order Convergent Memory.** These questions involve identifying, naming, defining, designating, and responding with "yes" or "no." Keywords might include *who, what, where, when*. Example: Name the capital of California.

» **Level II: High Order Convergent.** These questions involve explaining, stating relationships, comparing, and contrasting. Keywords might include *why, how, in what way*. Example: Explain how photosynthesis works.

» **Level III: Low Order Divergent.** These questions involve predicting, hypothesizing, inferring, and reconstructing. Keywords might include *imagine, suppose, predict, if/then*. Example: What might have happened had oxygen been introduced to the experiment?

» **Level IV: High Order Divergent.** These questions involve valuing, defending, judging, and justifying choices. Keywords might include *defend, judge, justify*. Example: Why do you think Harry Potter is such a good book series?

COSTA'S THREE LEVELS OF QUESTIONING

Costa's Three Levels of Questioning break down questioning into three parts (Brulles & Brown, 2018; Costa & Kallick, 2008; Edward R. Murrow High School, n.d.):

» Level 1: Gathering,
» Level 2: Processing, and
» Level 3: Creating.

Level 1 questions are designed to have student gather information. They are lower level questions because students use their short-term memory to answer. Without using the information in a meaningful way, students may forget it (Edward R. Murrow High School, n.d.). Gathering level questions usually involve one of the following actions:

» defining,
» describing,
» identifying,
» listing,
» naming,

» observing,
» reciting, or
» scanning (p. 1).

Level 2 is the processing level. This involves students taking something they have learned and making sense of it. This involves the skill of applying. This is the midrange of thinking. It shows that students know how to use the information, which is a sign of the information moving from short-term memory to long-term. Students are beginning to understand but are still just using the information in its basic form. Processing level questions usually involve one of the following actions (Edward R. Murrow High School, n.d.):

» analyzing,
» comparing,
» contrasting,
» grouping,
» inferring,
» sequencing, or
» synthesizing (p. 1).

Level 3 questions require students to go beyond the basic understanding of what they have learned and use their knowledge in a new situation. Creating level questions usually involve one of the following actions (Edward R. Murrow High School, n.d.):

» applying,
» evaluating,
» hypothesizing,
» imagining,
» judging,
» predicting, or
» speculating (p. 1).

Costa's Three Levels of Questioning are a good way to categorize the types of questions you are asking. The levels are a great place to start if you are at the beginning of your question forming process. Costa's system is a little limited in that two-thirds of questions are categorized as lower level, but only one-third higher level. As you begin to get deeper, however, having a system that provides more higher level choices can be helpful and provide you more nuance to your questioning.

WEBB'S DEPTH OF KNOWLEDGE

Another option is Webb's (1997, 2002) depth of knowledge (DOK) model, which describes four levels of cognition:
» DOK Level 1: Recall,
» DOK Level 2: Skill/Concept,
» DOK Level 3: Strategic Thinking, and
» DOK Level 4: Extended Thinking.

As you can see, DOK Level 1 is a simple recall of knowledge. It typically involves working with facts, but involves little if any transformation or extended processing of these facts. Students either know the answer to a DOK 1 question, or they do not. It is not something that can be figured out. DOK Level 1 involves:
» explaining simple concepts,
» recalling a fact,
» basic calculations,
» describing something that is seen, or
» identifying elements in a reading passage (Northern Indiana ESC, n.d., p. 1).

DOK Level 2 is the application of that knowledge. Instead of merely recalling what was learned, someone in this level would be able to apply it, maybe even to a new situation. An example would be if students learned the spelling rule "I before E except after C" using the word *believe*. They would then be able to apply this same concept to different words they were previously not exposed to, such as *friend*, *piece*, or *receive*. DOK Level 2 involves:
» solving multistep problems,
» showing relationships,
» applying a concept,

» identifying patterns, or
» predicting a logical outcome (Northern Indiana ESC, n.d., p. 1).

DOK Level 3 is more open-ended, requiring reasoning and strategic thinking. DOK Level 3 involves:

» interpreting information,
» looking at the big picture through concepts,
» developing a logical argument that is supported with details and examples,
» solving nonroutine problems, or
» finding a solution but also being able to justify it (Northern Indiana ESC, n.d., p. 2).

Finally, DOK Level 4 is about extended thinking, taking time to process and evaluate as students go deeper into an investigation. Most assessments do not include DOK 4, but this level should be where you ultimately want students to be able to go with their thinking. DOK Level 4 involves:

» critiquing to make something better,
» connecting common themes across subject matters,
» making conclusions from several sources of information,
» taking an idea and developing a new concept from it, or
» considering multiple strategies for tackling a problem (Northern Indiana ESC, n.d., p. 2).

When using the DOK Levels, you must properly identify your questions so that you can determine whether you are asking enough of the higher levels, DOK 3 and 4. A question's DOK level:

» should reflect the level of thought students are required to perform;
» should reflect the complexity of the thinking demanded by the question, rather than its difficulty; and
» should be assigned based upon the cognitive demands required by the question (Mississippi Department of Education, 2009).

DOK levels have become more popular in recent years for understanding the levels of thinking we are asking of our students. Because of this, you will find a lot of supplemental material to help you when using the DOK model.

FUSCO'S QUESTIONING STRATEGIES

We can categorize questions into three types, according to Fusco (2012): (1) literal questions, (2) inferential questions, and (3) metacognitive questions. Literal questions can be answered using specific responses that employ recall and fact. Literal questions typically cannot be disputed or argued. They are either correct or not. Examples might include:

» How many pounds are there in a kilogram?
» Who is the Spaniard credited with discovering Florida?
» What does a decomposer do in the food chain?
» Why would someone use a pronoun?

Answers to these questions are possible when students are exposed to the information and can recall it later. There is a lot of teacher control with this type of learning because it requires the teacher to either provide the answer or a resource that exposes students to it. Students then react to the question, trying to trigger their memory to access the knowledge.

Inferential questions are not directly stated (Fusco, 2012). Students have to connect the dots rather than simply recall the information. These questions tend to be open-ended, although some will have definite answers that must be determined, not recalled. With this type of learning, students have to develop their own form of reasoning to be able to arrive at a conclusion. These conclusions are usually fairly logical and do not require much imagination. Examples might include:

» If you have a dumbbell that weighs 20 kg, what would the approximate weight of the dumbbell be in pounds?

» How is the discovery of Florida by the Spanish still present in modern times?

» What happens if you do not have a decomposer in an ecosystem?

» Why would it be bad if the author of a novel chose not to use any pronouns?

Metacognitive questions involve students using what they know, connecting information to their own lives, and providing context for why it is important for them to learn it (Fusco, 2012). These questions are designed to build cognitive skills by making students aware of their needs and processes, thus the name *metacognitive*. Examples might include:

» Why should you know how to convert weights to kilograms?

» How have encroaching cultures influenced your culture?

» Is there a decomposer in the ecosystem you currently exist within, and what role does it play in your life?

» What pronoun do you most identify with, and why?

Metacognitive questions are proactive and are often asked by the students themselves. They naturally develop from questions like "Why are we learning this?", "What does this have to do with my life?", and "How does this influence my thinking?"

Fusco's (2012) metacognitive level of questioning can be powerful for three reasons. First, this level of questioning is authentic because it builds real-world connection to students' lives. A lot of other types of questions do not. Many are more artificial, created for the purposes of learning but without opportunities for students to see how concepts directly affect them. Second, this level of questioning inspires students' thinking and increases their motivation to answer because of these real-world connections. Third, this level of questioning builds students' reflection skills. Reflection can be a very powerful way to learn. Thinking about why they are learning what they are learning will better help students make connections, resulting in stronger learning and retention.

You should choose a questioning system that makes sense for you and your classroom. You will often need to generate questions in real time and will need to be able discern the level at which you are asking students to think almost instantaneously. There are other instances, such as written assessments or planned classroom discussions, for which you will have more time to generate an appropriate ratio of higher to lower level questions. But having a system that works for you will help you ensure that you are effectively challenging students and allow you to collect better data. When choosing a questioning system, consider the strategies outlined in this chapter, the needs of your students, and the reflection questions at the end of this chapter.

REFLECTION QUESTIONS

1. How comfortable are you with discerning the levels of questions you ask in your classroom?
2. What strategies can you use to improve your abilities to generate higher level questions?
3. Why are open-ended questions important for learning? Do you feel that you utilize enough open-ended questioning in your current classroom environment?
4. Why is it important that students be able to connect learning to their own lives? What are some ways you can build real-world connections into your questioning practices?

Chapter 4

Using Bloom's Taxonomy to Improve Your Questioning Behavior

Essential Question

How do you effectively use verbs to
vary levels of student thinking?

Chapter 3 presented five systems you could use to classify and structure questions. Any one of them would work well on its own or in combination, provided you have a clear understanding of the strategies. For the purposes of this chapter, I am going to focus on the system that helped me become a better questioner: Bloom's (1956) taxonomy. I like Bloom's taxonomy because I found it easier to identify the level of questions with the help of suggested verbs. In most cases, there are specific verbs associated with each level of Bloom's taxonomy. In other words, if a question asks students to *name* who the president of the United States is, this question falls clearly under the remembering level of Bloom's taxonomy, in which students are tasked with simple recall of a fact. If, on the other hand, the question asks students to *judge* whether a president made the correct decision or not, then the question is at the evaluating level. In addition, I have taught in gifted education for most of my career, which means that I need even more possibilities for differentiation. Bloom's taxonomy provides six different levels at which you can ask questions, providing plenty of room to raise the rigor for students.

BLOOM'S TAXONOMY

Bloom's taxonomy was named for Benjamin S. Bloom. It was developed in 1956 and followed the work Bloom had completed on the three domains of learning:

» **Cognitive:** The knowledge-based domain, consisting of six levels.
» **Affective:** The attitudinal-based domain, consisting of five levels.
» **Psychomotor:** The skills-based domain, consisting of six levels.

Bloom's taxonomy deals specifically with the cognitive domain. Originally developed for use by university professors, it quickly became used by curriculum planners, administrators, researchers, and classroom teachers at all levels of education (Anderson & Sosniak, 1994, p. 1). It continues to be taught to upcoming teachers as one of the leading models for critical thinking skills.

Bloom's (1956) taxonomy involves breaking the cognitive domain into six parts:
1. knowledge,
2. comprehension,

3. application,
4. analysis,
5. synthesis, and
6. evaluation.

Notice that these are all nouns. Eventually, a former student of Bloom, named Lorin Anderson, led a team in the 1990s to update the taxonomy. The "new" Bloom's taxonomy was published in 2001 and made one major change (Anderson & Krathwohl, 2001). Instead of nouns, the new Bloom's taxonomy utilized verbs because verbs describe actions, and it is important to remember that thinking is an active process. The revised labels of Bloom's taxonomy (see Figure 6) are:
1. remember,
2. understand,
3. apply,
4. analyze,
5. evaluate, and
6. create.

Each level is described in depth throughout the following sections.

REMEMBER

The remember level of Bloom's taxonomy is considered to be the lowest level and is probably the one that educators are the most familiar with and also, unfortunately, use the most. The remember level involves recalling facts, terms, basic concepts, and answers, such as when a teacher asks students to name important dates they have memorized or answer basic literal questions.

Examples for each of the content areas might include:
» **Social Studies:** Recalling the names of the seven continents.
» **Math:** Memorizing all of the multiples of 9 up to 108.

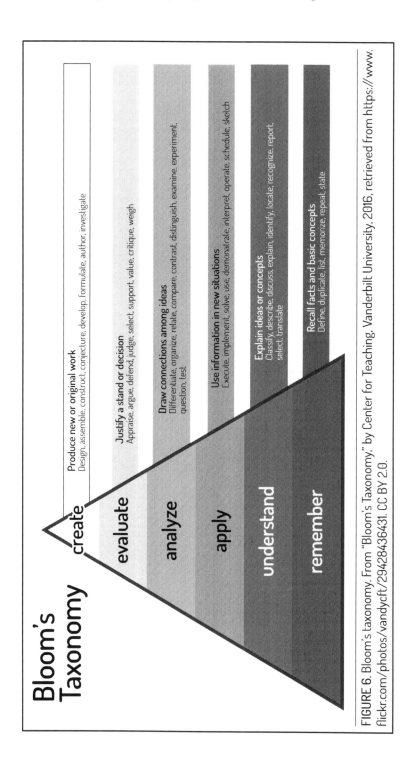

FIGURE 6. Bloom's taxonomy. From "Bloom's Taxonomy," by Center for Teaching, Vanderbilt University, 2016, retrieved from https://www. flickr.com/photos/vandycft/29428436431. CC BY 2.0.

» **Language Arts:** Knowing the common conjunctions of *and*, *but*, and *or*.

» **Science:** Recognizing elements on the periodic table.

Verbs associated with this level include:

» identify	» recall
» describe	» tell
» name	» reproduce
» select	» define
» locate	» list

Keep in mind that just because questions are the lowest level of the taxonomy does not mean that they are not important. Remember level questions are the starting point for any learning, higher or lower level. You cannot support higher level questions without a foundation of knowledge and understanding built through remember level questioning. You just need to make sure that you still go beyond the remember level if you want to raise the level of rigor in your classroom. There are many appropriate times to use remember level questions, such as when:

» reviewing material already learned,

» introducing a concept by starting with definitions,

» teaching basic math facts that will be used later to develop more advanced math skills,

» something has to be memorized, or

» determining whether something is true or false.

UNDERSTAND

Understand is the next level in Bloom's taxonomy. This level of cognition builds upon students' basic knowledge by asking them to explain what they know. Keep in mind that this level of cognition does not involve students creating a new product, but rather, proving that they understand what they have learned. This could include having students summarize their understanding of a reading or recent lesson. This level requires organization of the facts and students' ability to explain them. The understand level builds upon the remember level because students need to respond in their own words rather than recite facts verbatim. Students must develop understanding before they can move on to the next level of cognition. If they do not possess an understanding, information might be misinterpreted or directions might not be followed. Questions at the understand level can also act as checkpoints to determine when students are ready to move on to new content.

Examples for each of the content areas might include:

» **Social Studies:** Concluding the result of what certain events caused.
» **Math:** Comparing shapes to one another.
» **Language Arts:** Restating the general plot of a story.
» **Science:** Organizing data collected during an experiment.

Verbs associated with this level include:

» interpret	» compare
» exemplify	» explain
» classify	» give examples of
» summarize	» illustrate
» infer	» outline

Notice that *infer* at the understand level means displaying understanding of information that might not be explicitly stated, such as reading a passage that states, "His face was red and his brows were knitted together," and concluding that the character is angry. *Interpret* at this level might involve students rewording a statement without presenting new information.

There are many appropriate times to use understand level questions, such as when:

» determining whether students have comprehended a reading,
» having students explain what they have learned to a classmate in their own words,
» checking whether students understand the major takeaways from a lesson,

» you want students to draw a conclusion from the information they have been given, or

» requiring students to show their work in a math problem.

APPLY

The apply level of Bloom's taxonomy involves students putting into practice what they have learned. Application is often referred to as the higher level of lower level thinking because it requires that students use their knowledge and understanding in order to solve problems they have not seen before. For example, if students are learning subtraction and are presented with a problem they have not yet been exposed to, can they solve it with what they know about subtraction? If they are able to solve it, then they are taking their understanding to an independent level of application beyond just reciting what they have learned.

Examples for each of the content areas might include:

» **Social Studies:** Using research skills to conduct a research project and independently find and cite information.

» **Math:** Classifying numbers as fractions, improper fractions, or mixed numbers.

» **Language Arts:** Developing an essay using the introduction, body, and conclusion structure.

» **Science:** Using the scientific method to independently conduct an experiment.

Verbs associated with this level include:

» solve	» illustrate
» apply	» examine
» produce	» model
» modify	» translate
» complete	» predict

You will likely use the apply level a lot when asking students to demonstrate that they have learned a concept through practice.

Because it seems as though students are using higher level thinking skills in order to apply a concept, many teachers are satisfied with getting students to this level. This, however, is not good enough if you truly want students to access higher order thinking. In order for this to happen, students need to be able to create. That is what the higher three levels of Bloom's allow students to do. That said, reaching those higher levels is not possible without application.

There are many appropriate times to use apply level questions, such as when:

» checking whether students understand a math concept by giving them additional problems to solve,

» having students follow rules of writing or grammar when composing a piece,

» seeing if students can take something they have learned and apply it to a new situation,

» asking students to use established formulas to covert/solve a problem, or

» asking students to use logic to predict the outcome of a situation.

ANALYZE

The analyze level asks students to dig a little deeper into what they are learning. It involves not just scratching the surface of what they are learning, but rather taking a closer look at it from different angles. When students analyze something, they do more than just provide an answer that is implicit or implied. They bring their own thinking into play, which is what makes analysis a higher order thinking skill. This level of cognition involves higher order thinking because students are not only understanding knowledge, but also bringing their own judgment into it. This allows students to distinguish between fact and opinion. This also will naturally lead to the next level of Bloom's taxonomy—evaluation.

Examples for each of the content areas might include:

» **Social Studies:** Studying the stock market and trying to predict what a stock will do based on its past performance and the future market.
» **Math:** Investigating the various steps in an incorrect problem and determining where the work went wrong and how to fix it.
» **Language Arts:** Connecting a character's motives to something that happened in the past.
» **Science:** Analyzing the relationships between different animals in an ecosystem.

Verbs associated with this level include:

» compare and contrast	» relate
» simplify	» transform
» conclude	» differentiate
» assume	» explore
» correlate	» prioritize

Being able to analyze a concept allows students to understand its organizational structure and components. This, in turn, allows students to see the big picture effects of a concept. When students are learning a new concept, they often have difficulty seeing it in context or how it fits into the grand scheme of what they are learning. Being able to successfully analyze takes students' thinking to a higher level and helps with a more enduring understanding because they can fully understand how a concept works.

There are many appropriate times to use analyze level questions, such as when:

» a large concept needs to be broken down into smaller parts,
» building understanding of the big picture or essential question of a concept,
» comparing and contrasting concepts or a concept's components,
» asking students to make connections between ideas or organize them, or
» getting students to begin to ask questions for themselves.

EVALUATE

The evaluate level of Bloom's taxonomy often asks students to state their opinions, which is why it can be considered one of the easier levels of higher order thinking. This level of cognition is about more than students just stating their opinions, however. It is also about how students defend their opinions. This means that students need to not only understand the "what" behind a concept, but also be able to understand the "why" and how to articulate it. Asking questions at the evaluate level in ways that require students to explain their opinions is incredibly important.

Examples for each of the content areas might include:

» **Social Studies:** Ranking the top 10 contributions from the Renaissance.
» **Math:** Judging whether a student chose the best method of solving a problem.
» **Language Arts:** Defending the actions of the character Severus Snape in the Harry Potter series.
» **Science:** Deciding whether or not a scientist acted ethically in his or her experiments.

Verbs associated with this level include:

» support		» rate
» prove		» recommend
» evaluate		» assess
» criticize		» argue
» debate		» choose

Evaluating is usually the easiest cognitive level for students to accomplish and the most fun. It can be helpful to provide a structure for students to share their opinions, whether that be during a debate, a mock trial, discussion, editorial, podcast, or other outlet for sharing their thoughts. Keep in mind that follow-up questions are crucial because students need to take the extra step of explaining their evaluations. They must really think about their opinions, why they are valid, and how they can appeal to others to agree with or understand their views. This is a valuable skill for them to possess.

There are many appropriate times to use evaluate level questions, such as when:

» discussing a controversial topic,
» debating two or more sides of an argument,
» having students justify an opinion or recommendation about something,
» asking students to self-evaluate themselves or reflect, and
» requiring students to back up their responses with well-informed evidence.

CREATE

The create level of Bloom's taxonomy asks students to put elements together to form a coherent whole. Sometimes this means reorganizing elements into a new pattern or structure using planning. Creating can be the most difficult of the levels to do with students because creativity can often fall to the wayside in the classroom in favor of comprehension. How often do students create something new in social studies or in math class? Many assignments and assessments involve hunting for a single correct answer. Educators need to do a better job of asking questions that allow students to create.

Examples for each of the content areas might include:

» **Social Studies:** Devising a solution to the housing shortage in third-world countries.
» **Math:** Constructing a strategy for counting the number of jelly beans in a jar.
» **Language Arts:** Rewriting the ending of a story so that it is more realistic.
» **Science:** Formulating an alternative hypothesis based on evidence.

Verbs associated with this level include:

» design	» improve
» invent	» build
» substitute	» produce
» imagine	» revise
» plan	» write

In order to successfully engage with this level of cognition, students must have the mindset that they can create through their responses and thinking. They can display creativity through the generation of new ideas, products, or ways of looking at things. You must provide time and space for students to be creative. You must challenge them to create with your questioning and then get out of their way as they start to do so. Creating is the highest, most advanced level of Bloom's taxonomy and one that students should be using consistently.

There are many appropriate times to use create level questions, such as when:

» asking students to generate new ideas,
» having students solve a problem by proposing solutions,
» having students improve plans that have flaws,
» you want students to use their creativity, and
» asking students to think of multiple possibilities.

Understanding each of level of Bloom's taxonomy is really important when it comes time to write or ask your own questions. You cannot ask a higher level question if you cannot recognize a higher level question. Having a firm understanding of the questioning system you decide to use will make it so much easier to differentiate your own questions.

REFLECTION QUESTIONS

1. Do you often ask questions from all levels of Bloom's taxonomy? How can you improve your questioning practices to ensure you are covering all levels?

2. How does a system such as Bloom's taxonomy allow one to differentiate the types of questions asked in the classroom? Why is differentiating questions important?

3. Are you cognizant of the verbs you use when asking questions? What could you do to improve the verbs you use?

4. How proficient are you at matching the kinds of questions you ask to the activity or the goal you want students to accomplish?

5. How often do you ask students to create in your class? What are some ways you can allow them to create more?

Chapter 5

Moving Questions Into a Higher Level of Thinking

Essential Question

How do you adapt lower level questions into higher order thinking?

Because educators tend to ask mostly lower level questions in the classroom, determining ways to bolster these questions so that they become higher level questions is crucial. Fortunately, you can use the questions you already ask and find ways to move them into higher levels of thinking. You can use Bloom's (1956) taxonomy to guide you from lower to higher levels of questioning and provide the structure to raise the rigor in the classroom. You can scaffold questions toward higher level thinking or to take lower level questions and transform them into higher level ones. This chapter shares a few strategies for adapting lower level questions into higher order levels.

SCAFFOLDING QUESTIONS

Consider your everyday questioning practices. Now imagine that you are building a scaffold, putting each question on a tier so that each question builds upon the one before it. You cannot climb a flight of steps without first hitting the bottom ones, and the same applies to Bloom's taxonomy. The better you understand the lower levels of thinking, the easier it will be to achieve the higher level ones. Figure 7 is a visual of this process.

You can start by asking students a remember level question to form a base of knowledge, and then ask additional questions to lead to higher thinking. If you were teaching about Goldilocks and the Three Bears, you could start at the lower end of thinking and build up:

- » **Remember:** What are items used by Goldilocks while she was in the Bears' house?
- » **Understand:** Explain why Goldilocks liked Baby Bear's chair the best.
- » **Apply:** What would Goldilocks use if she came to your house?
- » **Analyze:** Compare this story to reality. What events could not really happen?
- » **Evaluate:** Judge whether Goldilocks was right for entering the Bears' house. Defend your opinion.
- » **Create:** Imagine how the story would change if you moved the setting from the woods to the ocean.

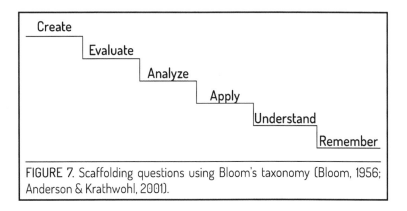

FIGURE 7. Scaffolding questions using Bloom's taxonomy (Bloom, 1956; Anderson & Krathwohl, 2001).

Here is a more advanced math example, using this learning objective:

Tell and write time from analog and digital clocks to the nearest 5 minutes, using a.m. and p.m.

You might begin with a simple remember level question such as this:

Identify the time on this clock.

If students answer with 10:10, then they have displayed their ability to tell time from an analog clock. This exercise can be taken a step further by asking students to understand:

If it were dark outside, distinguish whether
the time would be a.m. or p.m.

Yes, a student could make an argument for a solar eclipse or for a city in Alaska, but the most logical answer would be a.m. because it is likely nighttime. Through this exercise, students show that they understand the difference between a.m. and p.m., as well as the 12-hour clock.

In order for students to apply this skill, you need to have them create.

Illustrate 2:35 on the clock provided.

Rather than having students look at a clock and tell you the time, they would have to independently indicate the correct time on the clock. They have to remember what the long and short hands indicate, as well as which number represents the 35-minute interval. You could make it a little more challenging by asking students the following:

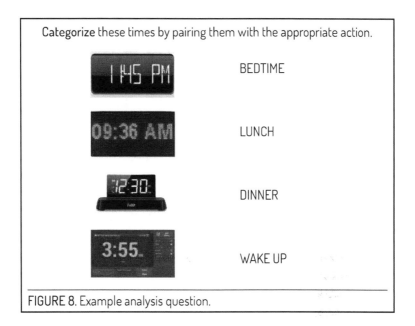

Categorize these times by pairing them with the appropriate action.

BEDTIME

LUNCH

DINNER

WAKE UP

FIGURE 8. Example analysis question.

Draw an analog clock that displays 2:35.

Through this exercise, students have to access more of their remember level skills, such as the numbers and spacing on a clock, and apply them. This task requires more thinking, but students are not at higher order thinking quite yet. You have to get them to think in more depth to accomplish this, such as through the question in Figure 8. This question requires students to analyze all of the possibilities before making their choices. Some things students would need to consider include:

» What is the time shown on the clock?
» Is the time shown in a.m. or p.m.?
» Around what time do the actions usually take place?
» Which time matches closest to each of the actions?

Consider the evaluate level question in Figure 9. There is no definitive answer. Students could make an argument for an 8 o'clock bedtime if they get up early in the morning. They could make a case for the 11:30 bedtime because this allows them to watch their favorite 10 o'clock television program and then get

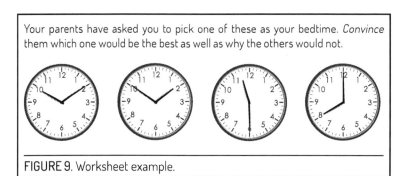

Your parents have asked you to pick one of these as your bedtime. *Convince* them which one would be the best as well as why the others would not.

FIGURE 9. Worksheet example.

ready for bed. The most logical answer is the 10:10 time, but it is by no means the only choice. Students must make a judgment and then convince others about their way of thinking.

Although the questions in Figure 8 and Figure 9 have asked students to think, they have not asked them to create something new. This question would:

Invent a game in which those participating must use the correct time in order to succeed.

Students would have to think about a way for someone to learn about telling time through a game. One idea might be to develop a game similar to the card game War. Instead of regular playing cards, the cards could be labeled with times. To play, players turn over a card from their stack. Then, a third card is turned over from a neutral stack. Whichever time is closest to the neutral card time wins that round, and the other player must add all of the cards from the round to the bottom of their stack. At the end of 15 minutes, whomever has the pile with the fewest cards wins the game. Students have created a game that allows someone playing it to use and understand the skills addressed in the learning objective.

All of these questions can be used to demonstrate that students understand how to read a clock. However, each level asks students to think more in depth about the skill. Each question or activity builds on the last, just as students build their depth of thinking.

Another strategy to consider is asking follow-up questions that scaffold students' thinking, much like using the Socratic method. You could take the first question and build on it with follow-up questions, each one moving up Bloom's taxonomy. The exchange might look something like this:

Teacher:	Who is the main character? (Remember.)
Student:	Jay Gatsby.
Teacher:	What makes you say that? (Understand.)
Student:	Because the story is about him. He's the protagonist.
Teacher:	What evidence from the book do you have to support that? (Apply.)
Student:	The book is all about him. It is even named after him. His actions drive the story. From his pursuit of Daisy to his death at the end, the story arc follows his life.
Teacher:	Why isn't Nick the main character? After all, he is the narrator, and all of the action occurs from his viewpoint. (Analyze.)
Student:	Because he is just in the background. He doesn't know what he wants, but Gatsby is very focused. He is determined to get Daisy back. Nothing that Nick does really affects the story. He is just watching it all happen in front of him as an impartial witness.
Teacher:	Do you think Gatsby is the right person to be the main character? (Evaluate.)
Student:	I don't see how the story could be told without him. He is the one character that can express the American dream Fitzgerald is satirizing because he is the only one that started poor but then became wealthy.
Teacher:	What would the story look like if Tom was the main character? (Create.)

Student: The story could still be about the American dream being dashed, but it would have to focus on the fact that he once was a big football star and now he must settle for not being in the spotlight. Fitzgerald could do something with that.

A real-life exchange might not be as streamlined at this, and additional questions might be needed to prompt further thoughts from the student, but you get the general idea. You can start by asking lower level questions and use them to build toward higher level thinking.

TRANSFORMING LOWER LEVEL QUESTIONS INTO HIGHER LEVEL QUESTIONS

If you have determined that your questioning behavior does not result in enough higher order thinking in your classroom, you do not have to get rid of all of your former questions. There are several ways to adapt your questions.

CLOSE-ENDED VERSUS OPEN-ENDED

A good way to think about the difference between lower and higher level questions is by understanding that lower level questions tend to be close-ended in nature or only have a single, correct answer. Higher level questions tend to be more open-ended or have many possible answers.

The following are examples from each of the core subject areas. Each close-ended (CE) question has been adapted into a more open-ended (OE) question.

Language Arts:
» CE: Identify the verb in the sentence.
» OE: Can you have a complete sentence without a verb?

Math:
» CE: What are grouping symbols?
» OE: Why is it important to use grouping symbols?

Science:
» CE: What are some renewable energy resources?
» OE: Are renewable energy resources realistic for meeting the needs of the United States?

Social Studies:
» CE: What was the Trail of Tears?
» OE: Was there a better way the government could have negotiated or compromised with Native Americans than embarking upon the Trail of Tears?

For each open-ended question, students have to have an understanding of the concept/term before they can answer it. That means that although they are answering a higher level question, they are building upon their lower level thinking skills.

UPDATING VERBS

Sometimes transforming a lower level question can be as simple as updating the verb in the question:
» Lower Level: Choose which of the answers is correct.
» Higher Level: Debate which of the answers is correct.

This example involves a minor difference in wording, but a big change in students' thinking. If students are choosing between two answers, they just have to determine which one is correct based on previous knowledge. But, if they have to debate which answer is correct, they have to consider factors from both sides, create a feasible argument, and then communicate the reasoning for their choices.

Here are examples of how you could change the verb in various subject areas, transforming questions from lower level (LL) to higher level (HL) thinking:

Language Arts:
- » LL: Describe the setting of the book.
- » HL: Change the setting of the book.

Math:
- » LL: Solve the equation.
- » HL: Modify the equation.

Science:
- » LL: Explain how chemical changes work.
- » HL: Validate how chemical changes work.

Social Studies:
- » LL: Name three advances prehistoric people developed.
- » HL: Rank three advances prehistoric people developed.

Keep in mind that verb updates will not always be possible. You might find yourself having to rewrite a question completely or creating another from scratch. One tool that aids in the writing of higher level questions is the use of questioning stems.

QUESTIONING STEMS

Questioning stems are an effective and easy-to-use tool if you are not quite comfortable with asking higher level questions. Questioning stems can get you started. You just have to insert your topic or skill into the stem. Here is a stem for a remember level question: "Can you list four . . .?" From this stem, you can insert whatever you need to make a question:
- » Can you list four adverbs?
- » Can you list four oceans?
- » Can you list four planets?
- » Can you list components of the rule of four in mathematics?

There are many stems for each of the levels of Bloom's taxonomy, including the lower levels. Table 1 is a list of possible stems for each level.

Say, for example, you wanted to create a higher level question on photosynthesis at the evaluate level. You could use the stem "What would happen if . . .?" to help form the question: What would happen if carbon dioxide were not present in photosynthesis? Because the question stems in Table 1 are fairly general, they can be applied to most any subject area. However, it is helpful sometimes to have stems that are more specific to a particular subject area. Table 2 includes stems specific to math/science, and Table 3 includes stems specific to language arts. You can use these stems as a guide when writing questions for assessments or could even keep them handy when running a discussion and use them to help form questions.

QUESTION GENERATOR

Another option to consider is the Question Generator, which you can use to develop driving questions that will get students to use critical thinking. This was developed by educator Seth Jaeger (n.d.) and breaks question writing into five parts:
1. stem,
2. topic,
3. concept,
4. category, and
5. active verb.

Using a graphic organizer, you decide what to put in these categories in order to generate questions (e.g., In what ways did . . . the Great Depression . . . beliefs . . . sports . . . change). You might have to rearrange sections to turn it into a complete sentence, but it gives you the basic structure of a higher level question: In what ways did the Great Depression change Americans' beliefs about sports? You can populate the categories in any order,

TABLE 1
Question Stems for Each Level of Bloom's Taxonomy

Remember	▸ How would you define ...? ▸ How would you identify ...? ▸ Describe what happens when ...? ▸ Where is ...? ▸ Who was ...? ▸ When did ...? ▸ List the _____ in order. ▸ How did _____ happen? ▸ How would you describe ...? ▸ How would you show ...?
Understand	▸ How would you compare ...? ▸ Elaborate on.... ▸ What is the main idea of ...? ▸ Can you write in your own words ...? ▸ Can you provide an example of what you mean? ▸ What could be the reason for ...? ▸ What can you interpret from this graph? ▸ Which does not belong? ▸ What do you conclude of ...? ▸ Covert _____ to _____.
Apply	▸ Do you know another instance where ...? ▸ What would be the result if ...? ▸ How would you demonstrate ...? ▸ Explain how _____ works. ▸ How would you solve ...? ▸ Could you apply _____ to something from your own life? ▸ How would you use ...? ▸ What does _____ remind you of? ▸ Examine the effects of.... ▸ Collect 10 examples of....
Analyze	▸ What is fact; what is opinion? ▸ What conclusions can you draw about ...? ▸ What is the relationship between ...? ▸ How is _____ related to ...? ▸ Can you distinguish between ...? ▸ What ideas support the fact that ...? ▸ What evidence can you find ...? ▸ What inferences can you make about ...? ▸ What do you see as other possible outcomes? ▸ What assumptions do you make about ...?

TABLE 1. Continued

Evaluate	▸ Do you believe ...? ▸ What do you think about ...? ▸ Find the errors. ▸ How would you have handled ...? ▸ Judge the value of. ... ▸ Do you think _____ is a good thing or a bad thing? ▸ How would you feel if ...? ▸ Can you defend your position about ...? ▸ What would happen if ...? ▸ What changes to _____ would you recommend?
Create	▸ What would happen if ...? ▸ What advice would you give ...? ▸ What changes would you make to ...? ▸ Can you give an explanation for ...? ▸ Can you see a possible solution to ...? ▸ If you had access to all resources, how would you deal with ...? ▸ Propose an alternative. ▸ How else would you ...? ▸ Can you design _____ to ...? ▸ How many ways can you ...?

but by putting the five parts together you can create higher level thinking questions. You can use the Question Generator for free at https://www.sethjaeger.com/p/question-generator.html. You can either download the app from Google Play or use a Google spreadsheet to write your questions. This tool is a nice simple way to write questions that take student thinking to the next level.

REFLECTION QUESTIONS

1. Are you working with students who already know the basics and can immediately be asked higher level questions, or do they need to build some background knowledge first before tackling higher order thinking?
2. How comfortable are you with the possible answers you might get by asking more open-ended questions?

TABLE 2

Example Question Stems for Math/Science

Analyze	▷ If the pattern continues...? ▷ What is missing from the problem? ▷ What is the best estimate for...? ▷ Can you identify the different parts? ▷ What is the function of...? ▷ What idea validates...? ▷ What is the problem with...? ▷ How can you classify _____ according to...? ▷ Discuss the pros and cons of.... ▷ How can you sort the parts...?
Evaluate	▷ What data were used to make the conclusion...? ▷ Judge the value of... ▷ What criteria would you use to assess...? ▷ What fallacies, consistencies, or inconsistencies appear? ▷ Is there a better solution to...? ▷ Which most accurately...? ▷ What are the chances of...? ▷ Which statement is sufficient to prove...? ▷ Develop a proof of _____ and justify each step. ▷ Hypothesize what the outcome will be.
Create	▷ What ideas could you add to...? ▷ What solutions would you suggest for...? ▷ Can you see a possible solution to...? ▷ Can you create new and unusual uses for...? ▷ Can you formulate a theory for...? ▷ How would you test...? ▷ Can you construct a model that would change...? ▷ Devise a way to.... ▷ How would you improve...? ▷ How would you compile the facts for...?

3. Do you understand how questions can be formed using the proper verb or stem?

4. Do you typically find yourself building the complexity of thinking with each follow-up question you ask? How can you improve your skills in this area?

5. How much thought are you putting into the questions you ask students?

TABLE 3
Example Question Stems for Language Arts

Analyze	‣ What is the theme of the book?
	‣ What persuasive technique was used?
	‣ Which events could not have happened?
	‣ How is _____ similar to _____?
	‣ If _____ happened, what might the ending have been?
	‣ Can you explain what must have happened when . . .?
	‣ What is the motive there?
	‣ What was the turning point in the story?
	‣ What does the author assume?
	‣ Diagram the plot of the story.
Evaluate	‣ Compare two characters in the selection. . . . Which was a better person . . .? Why?
	‣ Which character would you most like to spend the day with?
	‣ Do you agree with the actions of . . .?
	‣ Why was it better that . . .?
	‣ What choice would you have made about . . .?
	‣ How could you convince someone to read this book?
	‣ Did the author do a good job of setting tone?
	‣ How would you have handled events?
	‣ Would it have been better if the author did . . .?
	‣ How would you defend the actions of this character?
Create	‣ How could you change the plot . . .?
	‣ Suppose you could _____. What would you do . . .?
	‣ How would you rewrite the section from _____'s point of view . . .?
	‣ How would you rewrite the ending of the story?
	‣ Predict what might have happened if events in the book had been different.
	‣ How would you portray . . .?
	‣ Develop a script for. . . .
	‣ Role-play a scenario about. . . .
	‣ Restructure the roles of the main characters.
	‣ Draw a picture about the story.

Chapter 6

Raising the Rigor of Content Standards

Essential Question
Are you teaching standards at their intended levels?

For better or worse, most teachers are responsible for teaching the content standards to their students and ensuring that students have mastered them by the end of the year. One way to ensure that students have learned the standards is by asking them questions, either on an assessment, during discussion, or in some sort of performance. This chapter will help you ask questions that cover standards at their appropriate levels, as well as raise the rigor on them.

ARE YOU TEACHING TO THE LEVEL OF THE STANDARD?

A lot of times when we look at a content standard, we look at its content. For example, here is a sixth-grade math standard from the Common Core State Standards (CCSS; National Governors Association Center for Best Practices [NGA] & Council of Chief State School Officers [CCSSO], 2010b).

CCSS.MATH.CONTENT.6.NS.C.7.B. Write, interpret, and explain statements of order for rational numbers in real-world contexts.

Someone might read this and assume that it is asking students to know how to put rational numbers in order from lowest to greatest in a real-world situation. If you were to assess whether a student has learned this, you might ask a question such as, "Write a statement to express the fact that -3 °C is warmer than -7 °C." If a student were to go to the whiteboard and write -3 °C > -7 °C, a teacher might think the student has learned the standard. The problem is that to "write" is only one of the skills the standard asked for. It asked for students to:

1. write,
2. interpret, and
3. explain.

Although the task covered the first of these skills, it did not involve interpreting or explaining. The student has not fully demonstrated the standard. A more effective question would have asked students to further interpret and explain (e.g., "It must have been really cold that day," "-3 is greater than -7 because they are negative numbers, meaning the closer to 0, the warmer it would be.")

There are many times when teachers do not ask enough of their students. This results in not truly teaching students what a standard requires. Take a look at this eighth-grade English language arts content standard (NGA & CCSSO, 2010a):

CCSS-ELA-LITERACY.RL.8.2 Determine a theme or central idea of a text and analyze its development over the course of the text, including its relationship to the characters, setting, and plot; provide an objective summary of the text.

A teacher might have students reading *The Call of the Wild* and ask what the theme is. A student could explain that the theme is adaptability because Buck must adjust to the harsh weather and conditions of the wilderness. The problem here is that students have only engaged with the first part of the standard, which requires lower level thinking (apply). The standard, however, asks students to take it a little further in their thinking, to not only determine theme, but also analyze its development over the course of a story. If the teacher were to push back and ask, "Are there instances when Buck had to learn to adapt that took some time to develop over the course of the book?", such a question might cause students to pause and consider. Sure, there is the obvious example of the wild, but then a student raises her hand:

Student 1:	He had to adapt to man.
Teacher:	And what do you mean by that?
Student 1:	Well, over the course of his time in the wild, he had—I think—three owners.
Teacher:	Does anyone remember their names?
Student 2:	There's Perrault, that French mail driver, and then Thorton.
Student 1:	Yeah, those are the guys. And each one treated Buck differently, and Buck had to adapt to each one of them in order to survive.

This student has it. She not only understands the lower level skill of determining theme, but also can take it a step further and analyze the story for long-term themes. Imagine, however, that the teacher had been satisfied with the first answer—that simply determining the theme was good enough for her class. What if the students were taking a high-stakes state test at the end of the year and were asked to analyze a passage and explain its ongoing theme? The students might be able to get the surface level idea of the theme, but they may not be able to dig a little deeper and show that they can analyze it. An end-of-year assessment would be the wrong time to discover that you were not teaching a standard at the level(s) of thinking it asks for.

HOW TO DETERMINE THE LEVEL OF A STANDARD

How do you determine the level of thinking a standard is asking of students so that you know what types of questions to create to assess mastery? Follow the verb. Because you are now familiar with Bloom's (1956) taxonomy and the verbs used at various levels of cognition, you can use these very same verbs to determine a standard's level of thinking.

Here are some examples where the verb(s) used sets the thinking level(s) of the skill that is outlined:

CCSS-ELA-LITERACY.W.9-10.2 Write informative/explanatory texts to examine and convey complex ideas, concepts, and information clearly and accurately through the effective selection, organization, and analysis of content.
Verbs: write, examine, analyze
Levels of thinking: understand, analyze, evaluate, create

CCSS.MATH.CONTENT.7.SP.A.2 Use data from a random sample to draw inferences about a population with an unknown characteristic of interest. Generate multiple samples (or simulated samples) of the same size to gauge the variation in estimates or predictions

Verbs: use, inference, generate
Levels of thinking: analyze, create

Next Generation Science Standard: 5-PS1-2. Measure and graph quantities to provide evidence that regardless of the type of change that occurs when heating, cooling, or mixing substances, the total weight of matter is conserved.

Verbs: measure, graph
Levels of thinking: apply, understand

CCSS.MATH.CONTENT.HSG-SRT.D.11 Understand and apply the Law of Sines and the Law of Cosines to find unknown measurements in right and non-right triangles (e.g., surveying problems, resultant forces).

Verbs: understand and apply
Levels of thinking: understanding and applying

This process will not always work. There are standards in which there is no determining verb. In the following sixth-grade language arts standard, a verb is included, but it does not really determine the level of the thinking. Through the context of the entire standard, you can determine that this involves the apply level of cognition because the graphics, images, music, and sound are being added, not created or manipulated:

CCSS-ELA-LITERACY.SL.6.5 Include multimedia components (e.g., graphics, images, music, sound) and visual displays in presentations to clarify information.

Also consider the following second-grade math standard. This standard simply establishes what the content is, without saying at what level it must be learned:

CCSS.MATH.CONTENT.2.NBT.A.1a 100 can be thought of as a bundle of ten tens — called a "hundred."

Most often, however, standards include a verb, but the verb can be occasionally misleading as far as what level of thinking the standard really covers. You might encounter a verb that does not match the level of thinking, such as in this Next Generation Science Standard (NGSS Lead States, 2013):

2-ESS2-2. Develop a model to represent the shapes and kinds of land and bodies of water in an area.

The verb *develop* usually involves the create level of Bloom's taxonomy, and although students will need to create a model to demonstrate this skill, their thinking will only involve application with regard to what they know about shapes and the land and bodies of water they are studying.

This language arts standard is similar:

CCSS-ELA-LITERACY.RI.7.9 Analyze how two or more authors writing about the same topic shape their presentations of key information by emphasizing different evidence or advancing different interpretations of facts.

Because the verb *analyze* is used, you might expect this standard to address the analyze level of Bloom's taxonomy. When students analyze a piece of writing, they infer what the author means, a higher level of thinking. When you read the standard and carefully consider what it is asking of students, it falls more in line with the understand level of cognition. The standard is asking students to cull through two documents and identify key information each of them use, or to compare the way each of the authors interprets the facts. Students do not actively make any interpretations themselves—there is little to no reading between the lines. They are tasked with finding the information laid out by the authors and comparing the two works.

A standard can also appear to be written at a lower level but actually require higher order thinking. Take, for instance, the following science standard from the NGSS:

3-5-ETS1-1. Define a simple design problem reflecting a need or a want that includes specified criteria for success and constraints on materials, time, or cost.

The verb *define* aligns with the remember level of Bloom's taxonomy, but this standard does not ask students to define a term or define a formula. It asks students to problem solve. In defining their simple design problem, they have to take into consideration constraints on materials, time, and cost. How the teacher defines these constraints can make the design problem more rigorous and challenging. For example, if the teacher asks students to build a tower as high as they can, but they are only permitted to use 20 pieces of paper as their materials, this is going to require more ingenuity than if they were given craft sticks or building blocks to work with. Students will have to think about all of the ways they can manipulate the paper, how it might take several different forms within the one structure, and, because paper is not terribly sturdy, how to construct the tower with a strong base so it can support itself. There are a lot of things to take into consideration above and beyond "defining" the problem.

RAISING THE RIGOR IN A STANDARD

Just because a content standard is written at a certain level does not mean that is the level you must stop at. After all, if you want to provide rigor in your classroom, you need to challenge students above expectations. You want to find opportunities in which you can take a lower level standard and assess students with a higher level question. Take this math standard, for example:

CCSS.MATH.CONTENT.2.GA.1 Recognize and draw shapes having specified attributes, such as a given number of angles or a given number of equal faces. Identify triangles, quadrilaterals, pentagons, hexagons, and cubes.

This standard asks students to recognize and draw, as well as identify, which are all lower level thinking skills. This standard could be covered in a few questions, such as:

» Which of the following shapes is a triangle?
» Draw a pentagon and number how many sides it has.

These tasks fulfill the level of thinking for recognizing and drawing. What if you took this standard up a notch? What if you asked students the same basic skill, but at a higher order of thinking? Would that not raise the rigor in the classroom? After all, students not only have to know the basics, but also understand them well enough to understand the concept in a different capacity.

Could you ask a question like the following?

Draw the following four shapes and then decide which one does not belong and explain why this is—parallelogram, hexagon, triangle, octagon.

In this task, students will have to draw each of the shapes with the correct number of sides: This covers the standard as written, but now students have to look for the pattern to decide which one does not belong. The beauty of this question is that there is more than one possibility. One possibility is that given that a parallelogram has four sides, a hexagon six, and an octagon eight, the odd shape is the triangle with three sides, as it is the only shape with an odd number of sides. A student could also argue that the parallelogram is the one that does not belong because it is the only one of the shapes that, if you folded them all vertically down the middle, would not match up with its sides. Students have to analyze in order to answer the question, increasing the level of their thinking.

Also consider this fifth-grade language arts standard:

CCSS.ELA.LITERACY.SL.5.3 Summarize the points a speaker makes and explain how each claim is supported by reasons and evidence.

This standard asks students to use only facts—facts about the points the speaker made, facts about evidence to support the claim, and facts organized in a summary written in students' own words. This standard is definitely at the understand level of thinking. In order to raise the rigor, all you would have to do is ask for students' opinion about these facts. Do students agree or disagree with the speaker? Does the speaker make a strong argument, or are there details that could be added to make it much stronger? A higher level question might look like this:

> Summarize the points a speaker makes, and explain how each claim is supported by reasons and evidence. Decide whether you agree or disagree with this speaker, and justify your reasons why.

Adding opinion to the question takes it to the evaluation level in which students are going to have to tap into more complex thinking. This task will require them to go beyond just culling together the facts and, instead, think about and comment on these facts in a well-thought-out argument. This added layer of depth will help students gain an enduring understanding of the standard, rather than just a cursory one.

Taking a content standard and asking questions that move it up the levels of Bloom's taxonomy is going to add rigor to your classroom because you will no longer just be asking students to know and understand something. You will be asking them to take their understanding and knowledge of the content and evaluate and create.

REFLECTION QUESTIONS

1. What is your goal or purpose for asking questions? Your goal should help you determine what levels of questions you will ask.

2. Why should the thinking level of the content standard form the basis of your lesson/learning, not just the content itself?

3. How often do you ask students to go above and beyond what a content standard asks them to learn? How can you add more opportunities for students to think beyond the standards in your classroom?

Chapter 7

Writing Rigorous Questions

Essential Question
How do you construct rigorous written questions for assessments and everyday activities?

Written questions come in various forms, from bell ringers and exit tickets, to homework and worksheets, to essential questions and classroom activities, to reflection journals and assessments. This chapter discusses each of these and how your question writing might look when using them.

BELL RINGER

A bell ringer is typically a question students are presented with as they walk into the classroom. This question can:

- » act as preassessment,
- » review something from the day before,
- » act as a warm-up to the day's activities,
- » focus students,
- » aid in the transition into the start of class,
- » prepare students for a discussion, and
- » provide reflection on a previous activity.

Regardless of your purpose, bell ringers are a great way to ask higher level questions to immediately raise the rigor in the classroom. If students are presented with a higher order thinking question the moment they walk into the classroom, they know that expectations are high. It has set a proper tone.

Here are some examples of bell ringers:

- » **Math:** Is there ever a time that 5 + 5 does not equal 10?
- » **Language Arts:** Would you have made the same decision that the mother did in *The Monkey's Paw*?
- » **Science:** How do you think things would be different if a cure for polio was never discovered?
- » **Social Studies:** What do you know about World War II?

Notice that these questions are open-ended. The goal of a bell ringer is not necessarily to see whether or not students know something. The purpose of a bell ringer is to jumpstart their thinking. This is why providing open-ended questions can be a good way to raise the rigor and get students thinking at those higher levels.

EXIT TICKET

Exit tickets are a great end-of-class tool for discerning whether or not students have understood a lesson. Exit tickets act a formative assessment or a checkpoint to make sure students have learned a concept before you can move on to the next topic. You can provide an exit ticket question or questions at the end of class, and collect them as students leave for the day. Exit tickets can be used to:

» Check students' understanding by having them summarize key points from the lesson
» Verify that students can solve a problem or answer a significant question based on the lesson
» See if students can apply the content in a new way
» Emphasize the essential question for the day's lesson
» Create extensions for students who demonstrate mastery after the lesson
» Have students ask questions they still have about the lesson (The Teacher Toolkit, n.d., sec. 2)

Notice that although some of these, such as the first three, involve simple recall, others require a bit more thinking, such as emphasizing the big picture or essential question, creating extensions, or having the students generate their own questions.

You could even scaffold your exit tickets, asking two questions, one that starts at a lower level and a second one that raises the rigor. For example:

1. What is the difference between a physical and chemical change?
2. Pick a season and find examples of physical and chemical changes that occur during it.

With the first question, students have to display a basic understanding of physical and chemical changes, and the second question lets the teacher know just how well students understand as they have to analyze and apply their knowledge to a season of their choice.

HOMEWORK

Although I am not a huge proponent of homework, it can be valuable in that it allows students to practice a skill until they master it. In a math class, this might look like showing students how to multiply fractions and then giving them 20 questions for homework where they can practice putting their new skill into play. In Spanish class, this might look like having students study the conjugation of verbs, which will help them later when they go to construct sentences for themselves. In an English class, the teacher might assign 30 minutes of reading so that students can practice building vocabulary and reading fluency in the process.

Homework does not always have to be about practice, however. You can organize the homework to get students to think about something they will be doing the next day or lesson. Some educators enjoy a flipped classroom, where they ask thought-provoking questions as part of the homework that students can learn and research on their own, and then class can be devoted to discussing what students have learned. For instance, say that an English teacher is having students read and analyze the short story "A Sound of Thunder" by Ray Bradbury. Rather than just assigning the short story as homework and having a cold discussion the next day based on the reading, the teacher could provide students with four or five discussion questions that they can take home and think about, so that the conversation the next day is richer:

» Knowing the risks, would you want to travel back in time?
» Why do you think the changes to history were so subtle and not bigger ones?
» Do you believe in the butterfly effect?
» What happens when you "leave the path" in your own life? Are there actions that affect your future?

» Why the title "A Sound of Thunder"? What might this mean?

Rather than assign 20 practice problems for homework in math, what if, instead, you give students the five most difficult questions before leaving class? If they are able to get them all right, rather than forcing them to do 15 more questions of what they already know, give them a homework assignment that is going to challenge them by asking them to think more deeply. Maybe ask them a question like this: "Can you write 15 problems of your own that use the math concept we are learning? Try to make each question more challenging than the last." When the students come in the next day, you could work some of these problems up on the board or have students swap homework papers and work on a peer's questions. When you assign homework, consider not only what students could be practicing, but also what they could be thinking in more depth about.

WORKSHEETS

The term *worksheet* has become a bad word in education. When you assign students a worksheet, the task is often thought of as merely busywork. This could be because run-of-the-mill worksheets involves activities such as word searches, which do not really teach students; coloring, cutting, and pasting, which might develop motor skills but not any thinking; or fill-in-the-blank responses. Worksheets are not considered to be good teaching practice because:

Professional educators generally consider worksheets convergent materials. Worksheets can lead students to believe that there is only a single correct way to use them and worksheets require little, if any, higher-order thinking. . . . Worksheet-based curricula dampen enthusiasm for learning. (Bisol, 2015, p. 19)

There are, however, ways to make worthwhile worksheets that will challenge students and raise the rigor in your classroom. Figure 10 is an example of a worksheet that has questions designed to get students thinking. This worksheet asks students to be creative while designing a bedroom for a book character, but it does not just involve creating something. This worksheet also allows students to show what they know about the characters. Students will have to take content and descriptions from the book in order to complete their design. Students will have to take context clues and read between the lines to make their decisions about a bedroom that will be the best fit for the character that they choose. This activity involves accessing higher order thinking. There is even a follow-up question that asks students to justify the decisions they made.

ESSENTIAL QUESTIONS

Some teachers like to use an essential question for a lesson, especially if what they are teaching is a large concept or big idea that would be helpful to frame. An essential question helps students keep the learning in context and can answer the most important question students often have, which is "Why are we learning this?"

There are five things you will want to consider when formulating your essential question:

1. **Will it spark discussion and debate?** An essential question typically asks a controversial question that is not easily answered. Many times, it can involve an ethical issue that can have many viewpoints and opinions. Because of this, the question lends itself to debate, with arguments able to be developed for either side.

2. **Will it stimulate ongoing thinking and inquiry?** The point of this book is to get you to ask students questions that will require them to think. Your essential question

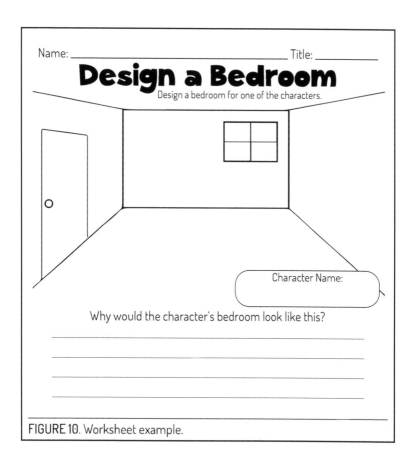

Name: _____ Title: _____

Design a Bedroom

Design a bedroom for one of the characters.

Character Name:

Why would the character's bedroom look like this?

FIGURE 10. Worksheet example.

should be thought provoking. An excellent essential question might have students thinking one thing when they start the lesson, but they could have a completely different point of view by the end.

3. **Will it raise further questions?** Just like Socrates showed through his methods, the best questions naturally lead to other questions. These follow-up questions drive the curiosity of students and develop their desire to learn more about a topic.

4. **Will it suggest multiple, arguable answers?** Essential questions are often open-ended and philosophical. They are not questions that have definitive answers—there might be several possible answers. Because there are sev-

eral sides, it is easy to use an essential question as a debate topic that will create lots of thought-provoking dialogue.

5. **Will it point to the lesson's big idea?** The essential question should capture the essence of a lesson. Because of this, the question has to have a broad scope. It cannot be so specific that the big idea gets lost. The essential question acts as the beacon for students, keeping them thinking about the focus of their learning.

An essential question should permeate the lesson, whether it is written on the board each day, appears at the top of any student handouts, is brought up in any discussions, or is referred to as much as possible. If the lesson is going well, students should not even have to refer to the essential question; it will just be present in everything they are doing toward their learning.

The following is an example of how you take a topic of learning and turn it into a big picture essential question. Consider this lesson introduction:

Topic: The semicolon
Lesson objectives:
» To have students understand what a semicolon is.
» To show students how to properly use a semicolon.
» To have students see the value of using this form of punctuation.

These objectives are not especially open-ended, nor do they require higher order thinking. Students might have even difficulty mustering up enthusiasm with the way this lesson is presented. However, consider if you provided students with this essential question:

Essential Question: Is the semicolon an essential form of punctuation in writing?

Suddenly, this lesson is interesting. Students will need to determine the value of the semicolon for themselves, rather than just being told by the teacher. Not only that, whichever way they decide, they will have to provide an argument for their point of view in order to answer the essential question. The level of thinking in this lesson has gone from the understand level of Bloom's taxonomy to the evaluate level. The rigor has been raised with a single question.

ACTIVITIES/DIRECTIONS

Even the written directions you give for activities can be phrased in a manner that will engage students in more higher order thinking. Take, for example, these directions to conducting a lab in science class:

Determine the Reactivity of Acids and Bases With Metals

1. Place a small sample of each metal to be tested in the different wells of a clean, dry microtray.
2. Use an eyedropper to add five drops of the hydrochloric acid onto each sample of metal. Note any signs of chemical change and record your observations in a data table.
3. Wash the miroctray and repeat steps 1 and 2 using the acetic acid.
4. Pay attention to the bubbles. What were the bubbles in the solution when the metals reacted with the acids? How do you think you could test to see what kind of gas was being produced in that reaction? Record your thoughts.

Notice that the first three steps of the directions are all about procedure. The fourth step, however, asks students to think about something, not just do it. The fourth step asks students to pay attention to the bubbles and ponder a couple of things about them. With this added direction, students will access higher levels of thinking, rather than just going through the motions of completing the lab.

Here is an example of directions for a social studies geography activity:

» Go to the interactive map found at https://demographics. coopercenter.org/united-states-interactive-map.
» Look at the estimated or projected population for the state of Texas for the years of 2010, 2020, 2030, and 2040.
» Think about possible causes for the increase in population over the decades.

The beginning set of directions walks students through where to look and what to do when they get there, but the last direction asks students to think. It is not even a question that requires a response—yet. In the third step, the teacher asks students to consider the possible causes while finding the information, which is something they might not have done without the guidance.

REFLECTION

Something educators do not do enough in the classroom is have students reflect on what they are learning. This means asking them their feelings and their thinking about what they are learning as much as possible. Reflection is a good way to challenge students to ask themselves what they truly "got" out of a lesson. If you are going to foster lifelong learners, your students need to be able to reflect upon their own strengths and weaknesses. Understanding their successes and failures when it comes to their learning is an important skill to possess. It is the only way students truly learn and improve their skills.

There are a couple of different ways you can organize purposeful reflection. One is by using prompts and having students reflect on them. Examples of prompts that promote higher order thinking include:

» What process did you go through during this lesson?
» In what ways have you gotten better at this kind of work? In what ways do you think you need to improve?

» What problems did you encounter while you were working on this lesson? How did you solve them?

» What was especially satisfying to you about either the process or the finished product?

» What were your goals for creating this piece of work? Did your goals change as you worked on it?

» What did you learn about yourself as you worked on this lesson?

» If you were the teacher, what comments would you make about your work?

» What's the one thing that you have seen in your classmates' work that you would like to learn from?

» What might you want next year's teacher to know about you (what things you're good at)?

» Think about another lesson that you did at the beginning of the year and compare and contrast it with this current lesson.

These prompts could be written on in a journal, typed up in a Google Doc, discussed amongst a group, or shared in a class discussion. The point is that not only should students be thinking, but also they should be thinking in ways that are introspective. More than that, they should be reflecting upon themselves and linking the lesson to their real lives, making their learning that much more authentic.

You can also conduct protocols. These are usually done as a group and start with a question that is either written on the board or on a sheet of paper. One such reflection tool might be a Chalk Talk, which can be used productively with any group. Because it is done completely in silence, it gives groups a change of pace and encourages thoughtful contemplation, and can be an unforgettable experience (Smith & Wentworth, 2019). Figure 11 is an example Chalk Talk protocol. I like this protocol because it has a double layer of reflection. The first aspect is reflection upon what you have done previously in class, whether it be a lesson, discussion, or idea. Then, after reflection on that, students reflect on the actual process of reflecting. All of the questions involve stu-

Chalk Talk

Time: 5–60 minutes depending on needs
Materials: White board and dry-erase markers, or chart paper and markers
Process:
1. Briefly explain that this is a silent activity. Students may add to the Chalk Talk with words or graphics. They can comment on other students' ideas simply by drawing a connecting line to the comment.
2. Write a list of relevant question in a circle on the board, for example:
   o   What did you learn today?
   o   What do you think about . . .?
   o   What did you learn about . . .?
   o   How is . . . used in the world?

3. When they have formulated ideas, students may write comments, ask questions, draw images/graphics, and show connections between various comments on the board.
4. Stand back and let the Chalk Talk unfold, or expand thinking by:
   o   circling interesting ideas,
   o   writing follow-up questions to comments,
   o   adding your own reflections/ideas, or
   o   connecting two corresponding/interesting ideas together with a line.

5. Ask follow-up questions as part of a discussion:
   o   What do you notice about what we wrote?
   o   What do you wonder about now?
   o   What was the Chalk Talk like for you?

FIGURE 11. Chalk talk example.

dents' opinions and allow them to explore what they think about a topic. The questions are open-ended and can elicit many different responses to the same question. You can check out other protocols for reflection on the School Reform Initiative website at https://www.schoolreforminitiative.org/protocols.

ASSESSMENTS

Assessment is usually associated with asking students written questions. Whether the questions be part of a formative or summative assessment, teachers usually formulate questions designed to determine student mastery. These questions can come in all sorts of different forms, whether they be multiple choice, true/false, fill-in-the-blank, short answer, or longer essays. The length of assessments also varies, from single-question tests to 100-question sets.

No matter what format you choose, you need to be aware of the levels of questions you ask. This means looking at the questions you are intending to include with the assessment and determining how many of them are asking students to think at a higher level. In a perfect world, an assessment would be half lower level, half higher level. That way you can use the lower level questions to gain an understanding of students' general mastery but also push students to delve a little deeper into the higher level questions. You can use what you know about scaffolding questions, question stems, and verbs in order to write higher order questions. Be aware of the ratio of higher level to lower level questions that you ask. One way to do that is through the use of a graphic organizer so you can track your work.

The taxonomy table (see Figure 12) is the perfect tool for this task. This graphic organizer allows you to record the content standards you are addressing with each question. Then, you can indicate what type of question is being asked (e.g., MC = multiple choice, SA = short answer, ER = extended response, GR = graphic response). If you are asking different formats of questions, you just need to adjust the categories on your graphic organizer. Then, the organizer is divided into the various levels of Bloom's taxonomy, divided into lower and higher level questions. You can determine the cognition level of each of your questions and record them on the organizer.

As you can see in the example in Figure 12, out of the 15 questions, there are only four that are in higher level range. Not only that, but there are zero questions that ask students to create. Fewer than a quarter of the questions ask students to think at a higher level. This is not a terribly rigorous assessment.

I noticed this lack of rigor in my own assessments. I thought I was challenging students by providing more essay questions than

Ques.	CS	MC	SA	ER	GR	Lower Level Ques.			Higher Level Ques.		
						Remb.	Under.	Appl.	Anal.	Eval.	Creat.
1.		X				X					
2.				X					X		
3.			X						X		
4.		X						X			
5.		X								X	
6.		X				X					
7.		X						X			
8.			X						X		
9.			X						X		
10.		X	X						X		
11.			X						X		
12.			X						X		
13.		X		X							
14.		X						X			
15.					X				X		

FIGURE 12. Taxonomy table example.

multiple-choice questions, but the way I was asking the essay questions did not require students to engage in higher level thinking. The questions were often only written to the apply level of Bloom's taxonomy. Once I began to track the ratio of higher level to lower level questions on my assessments and became more dedicated to higher order thinking, I realized I needed to make some revisions. For the example in Figure 12, the teacher would merely have to take three of the lower level thinking questions and modify them, changing the level of thinking. Writing higher level short answer responses is always easier than writing multiple-choice questions, so those two could easily be made more rigorous. The teacher could also take a couple of the graphic responses or multiple-choice questions and adapt them.

Awareness is the key to writing higher level assessments. You don't know what you don't know. If you don't know that you are asking too many lower level questions, you won't make any effort to change. Using a graphic organizer such as this makes you more aware so that you can change your practices and become a better teacher.

Hopefully, however, the pattern you have seen throughout this chapter is that higher level questions can—and should—be used in your classroom throughout the day-to-day activities that students are involved in. Higher level questions do not need to be reserved solely for discussions or major tests. The more you practice the use of higher level questions, the more comfortable students will become. This will begin to build a culture of inquiry and rigor in your classroom.

REFLECTION QUESTIONS

1. What written questions do you ask students on a day-to-day basis? Do they involve higher level or lower level thinking?
2. How much thought do you put into your written questions? What strategies can you employ to ensure that you are creating effective questions?
3. Are there areas in which you could raise the rigor by modifying questions to require more higher order thinking? What areas (e.g., assessments, essential questions, homework, etc.)?
4. If you could change something about written questions in your classroom tomorrow, where would you start?

Chapter 8

Asking Higher Level Verbal Questions

Essential Question
How purposeful are you about the questions you verbally ask students?

One big advantage of written questions is that you usually have time to sit down and prepare your questions ahead of time. You have all sorts of resources you can pull from in order to purposely and thoughtfully construct your questions to challenge students' thinking. You do not always have the luxury of time when asking verbal questions. Many times, they must be formulated and asked in a split second. This means you must think quickly on your toes, something you're well-versed in as a teacher. However, do not think that, just because the responses to your verbal questions are generally not graded, verbal questions are less important than written questions. In fact, your verbal questioning is the best way to raise the rigor in your classroom and get students accessing their higher order thinking skills.

CREATING AWARENESS

What is the best way to learn how to verbally ask great higher level questions at a moment's notice? Like any skill, it comes down to practice and awareness. The more you do it, the more comfortable you will be. You will start to recognize the ratio of higher level to lower level questions that you ask, building an effective balance. Being "aware" in the classroom can be difficult at times. You have 30-something students you are responsible for teaching. Often, this means focusing on surviving the day, which means sometimes overlooking smaller details. For instance, I once had to record a video of my teaching for my National Board application. As I rewatched the video, cringing at how awkward I was at times, I noticed something I had never noticed before; I was teaching predominantly to the right side of the room. As I spoke to the classroom, I tended to turn to my right and direct my instruction there. I was not blatantly turning my back on the left side of the classroom (they could hear what I was saying), but I was subtly sending a message that I thought the right side of the room was more important than the left. That, of course, was not the case, but the video made me aware of my actions. The next time I got up in front of the class to speak, I was cognizant of what side of the room I was talking to throughout. To prevent myself from over-compensating by just teaching to the left side of the classroom, I recorded myself again and made a concerted effort to address both sides of the room.

A similar occurrence happened when I was being observed by my principal for my evaluation. He sat in the back of my classroom, observing a discussion I was running. When we got together a couple of days later to reflect, the following conversation occurred:

Principal: Do you realize that you call on boys more than girls when running a discussion?

Me: What do you mean?

Principal: While you were conducting that discussion, you tended to call on boys raising their hands more than girls.

Me: Really?

Principal: Really.

Me: Were more boys raising their hands than girls?

Principal: No, it was pretty evenly distributed. But I noticed you called on one girl for every three boys.

This was shocking to me. Was I subtly discriminating against my students without knowing it? I decided to pay more attention to who I was calling on. I began to keep a tally the next time we had a discussion. Once I was aware of the issue and paying more attention, I found it easier to make sure I was giving each student opportunities to speak.

Data collection is important because you might think that students are really learning something well, but the data from their assessments may prove otherwise. As you know, being aware of the types of questions you are asking in your classroom is the first step toward asking more higher level questions. You can use a simple graphic organizer such as Figure 13 to track the types of questions you ask based on Bloom's taxonomy. You might notice that you ask one type less than another and overcompensate, so keep in mind that balance is key.

A different strategy might work better for you. For example, you could ask a colleague to sit in on your class and keep track of the types of questions you ask. Another option would be to record a video of you leading a lesson. This is always interesting in that you will see things you never realized before—maybe you

Level of Bloom's Taxonomy	How Many Times Has This Type Been Asked?
Remember	
Understand	
Apply	
Analyze	
Evaluate	
Create	

FIGURE 13. Question type tracker.

use "um" too often or spend too much time sitting at your desk. By recording a video, you will get an accurate idea of the levels of questions you ask your students, as well as an understanding of how you can improve your questioning.

PREPARING QUESTIONS AHEAD OF TIME

You can always prepare questions ahead of time. This will help you to become better at formulating questions on the spot because it will provide you with confidence. This strategy is known as scripting. How you decide to script is up to you, but I suggest you arrange your list of questions in a logical sequence, from lower level to higher. This way the scaffolding of questions can occur naturally. For example, if you are going to have a discussion on the purpose of government, you would want to come up with questions that would enable you to create a rich dialogue between students. This will involve a combination of lower and higher level questions. Your scripted questions might look like this:

» **Remember:** What is government?
» **Understand:** How does the government work?
» **Apply:** How does the government work for you?

» **Analyze:** How does our government compare with some other types of government?
» **Evaluate:** Do you think the government, in its current state, is effective?
» **Create:** If you could make your own government, what would it look like?

The way these questions are arranged, one question leads into the next, and they increase in the level of thinking with each one. The main goal in scripting your questions is to be organized enough that the questions cover the material you need to help students learn, as well as spark meaningful conversation about the topic.

While planning your questions you will want to try to anticipate possible student responses. Write these follow-up questions down so that you are ready when opportunities arise. Anticipating student responses should help in your planning by forcing you to consider whether your questions are any good. If you have to ask a follow-up question, is the question you are asking constructed in the best way possible? Does the question lend itself to a follow-up question that will deepen and enrich the discussion?

Here are follow-up questions to the original questions for a discussion on government:

» **Remember:** What is government? *How is it more than just politicians?*
» **Understand:** How does the government work? *Where have you seen instances of government in your day-to-day life?*
» **Apply:** How does the government work for you? *Do you feel there are instances where it doesn't work for you but should?*
» **Analyze:** How does our government compare with some other types of government? *Have you looked at the basic idea of communism, not how it is currently being used? Do you think that could work for people?*
» **Evaluate:** Do you think the government, in its current state, is effective? *What would you do to improve our current government?*

» **Create:** If you could make your own government, what would it look like? *What would the world look like without a government?*

These follow-up questions should push the conversation deeper, not quicker. In a good discussion, you want to slow down. This is when the higher order thinking takes place. If you are rushing through a discussion, hunting and pecking for correct answers, then you are missing an opportunity for rigor.

When scripting your questions here are a few things to take into consideration:

» Am I asking an open or closed question? What type of response do I expect from students? Is the question phrased in a way to allow this to happen?

» Do I have a good mix of questions on the full range of Bloom's taxonomy?

» What will I do if students answer differently than I expect? What is plan B?

» Do I have dead-end questions? These are questions that stop the progress of the discussion because there is nowhere to go with them.

» Do I have enough questions to sustain the discussion? You should always have more questions than you are going to actually use.

Keep in mind, when scripting, you do not want to allow the script to dictate the discussion. It is merely a guide. You should have enough flexibility to allow students to express ideas in their own words. You also need to be willing to let the discussion go where student interest takes it. Some people call that getting sidetracked. I call that learning.

COMING UP WITH QUESTIONS ON THE FLY

There will be many times you have to come up with questions on the spot. If you are not yet comfortable with this, what are strategies you can use to allow you to practice it and gain more confidence?

One method is carrying a taxonomy flip chart with you while leading a discussion. This way, when you have to form a question, you have something to help you do so. These charts usually contain the verbs associated with each level of Bloom's taxonomy, as well as question stems. (See Chapter 5 for question stems.) You can use the stems to create a question as needed, simply inserting the topic into the stem. Consider the government discussion used earlier in the chapter. Say that you have asked your scripted apply level question, as well as its follow-up:

Apply: How does the government work for you? *Do you feel there are instances where it doesn't work for you but should?*

The discussion is rich, and you want to maintain the rigor for your students, so you need to come up with a question that keeps the ideas flowing. You take one of your stems (What is the relationship between . . .?) and fill in the topic: What is the relationship between government and citizenship?

There are all sorts of tangential ideas students could explore with such a question:

» How do citizens use the government to their benefit?
» What is citizens' responsibility to their government?
» What if citizens decide the government is not working for them? Can they opt out of it?
» What is a citizen without a government? What is a government without a citizen?
» How do citizens and government work together to benefit the greater good? Can one work without the other?

Not only have you opened another line of questioning, but also you have raised the rigor in your classroom by taking the questions from the apply level to the analyze level. This will spark further discussion and allow students to use their higher order thinking skills.

Bloom's taxonomy flip charts are relatively inexpensive (around the $5 mark) to purchase, or you could just make your own using the verbs and questioning stems provided in this book. Another strategy is to have a list of general questions in your toolbox. These can be asked in almost any discussion and most times will elicit further dialogue and raise the rigor:

» Could you explain that in your own words?
» Could you give me an example of that?
» How do you know that is the correct answer?
» What part of this was the most difficult for you, and why?
» Can you think of any other reasons why this should be considered important?
» How will this lesson benefit you in the future?
» What was the most interesting thing that you learned?
» What made you think of it like that?
» Are there other ways to look at this?
» How does this apply to your own life?

THE IMPORTANCE OF FOLLOW-UP QUESTIONS

As discussed, follow-up questions can be a really good way to take students' thinking to a higher level. Teachers will often ask a question, get the response they are looking for, and then move onto the next. This misses a prime opportunity to explore some higher order thinking. You should continue to ask students questions until they arrive at a deeper understanding or are thinking about the topic in a new, different way. Use "How?" and "Why?" These prompts cause students to pause and think—something you want them to do.

Take, for instance, the simplest of questions: "What is your favorite color?" This questions requires almost no thinking, as most students have their favorite color in mind. Asking just requires students to recall what it is. If, however, you followed up with, "Why is that your favorite color?", then students have to give their selections more thought. Is there something associated with the color that makes it their favorite? Is there a pleasant memory the color brings up? Why does this color stand above other colors? This engages students in the evaluate level of Bloom's taxonomy. In answering this question, students have to construct criteria as to why their favorite color is so great. This thinking will not be instantaneous. Students will have to dig a little deeper and investigate their choices.

If you were to ask students, "What is 2 + 2?", they will quickly be able to tell you the answer is 4. Asking a follow-question, "How did you get that answer?", causes students to pause and consider what operation they are using to figure out the answer or how to explain in their own words how they arrived at the answer. This follow-up question asks students to think, not recite. This is what you want to accomplish with follow-up questions. As you get more comfortable, you will be able to move beyond "Why?" and "How?" questions, but they are certainly a good place to start.

STRATEGIES TO USE WHEN STUDENTS RESPOND

The tricky thing about asking questions is that students are going to give you answers. The question you have to ask yourself is: What are you going to do with these answers? You can choose to just accept them as is, but then that is kind of boring. Are there ways you can take student answers and get students to think at a higher level? Here are some suggestions provided by the Center for Innovation in Teaching & Learning at the University of Illinois (CITL, n.d.):

» **Reinforcement:** The instructor should reinforce student responses and questions in a positive way in order to encourage future participation. The instructor can reinforce by making positive statements and using positive nonverbal communication. Proper nonverbal responses include smiling, nodding and maintaining eye contact, while improper nonverbal responses included looking at notes while students speak, looking at the board, or ruffling papers. The type of reinforcement will be determined by:

- The correctness of the answer. If a student gives an answer that is off-target or incorrect, the instructor may want to briefly acknowledge the response, then think of ways to help the student provide a correct answer. The instructor could use strategies such as probing, paraphrasing, or asking the question in a different way.

- The number of times a student has responded. Instructors may want to provide a student who has never responded in class with more reinforcement than someone who responds often.

Be sure to vary reinforcement techniques between various verbal statements and nonverbal reactions. Try not to overuse reinforcement in the classroom by overly praising every student comment. Students begin to question the sincerity of reinforcement if every response is reinforced equally or in the same way.

» **Probing:** The initial response of students may be superficial. The instructor needs to use a questioning strategy called probing to make students explore initial comments. Probes are useful in getting students more involved in critical analysis of their own and other students' ideas. Probes can be used to:

- Analyze a student's statement, make a student aware of underlying assumptions, or justify or evaluate a statement. *Instructor:* What are some ways we might solve the energy crisis? *Student:* I would like to see a greater movement to peak-load pricing by utility companies. *Instructor:* What assumptions are you making about consumer behavior when you suggest that solution?

- Help students deduce relationships. Instructors may ask students to judge the implications of their statements or to compare and contrast concepts. *Instructor:* What are some advantages and disadvantages of having grades given in courses? *Student 1:* Grades can be a motivator for people to learn. *Student 2:* Too much pressure on grades causes some students to stop learning, freeze, go blank. *Instructor:* If both of those statements are true, what generalizations can you make about the relationship between motivation and learning?
- Have students clarify or elaborate on their comments by asking for more information. *Instructor:* Could you please develop your ideas further? Can you provide an example of that concept? *Student:* It was obvious that the crew had gone insane. *Instructor:* What is the legal definition of insane? *Student:* It was a violation of due process. *Instructor:* Can you explain why?

  » **Adjust/Refocus:** When a student provides a response that appears out of context, the instructor can refocus to encourage the student to tie her response to the content being discussed. This technique is also used to shift attention to a new topic. *Instructor:* What does it mean to devalue the dollar? *Student:* Um—I'm not really sure, but doesn't it mean that, um, a dollar doesn't go as far as it used to? Does that mean it's devalued? *Instructor:* Well, let's talk a little bit about another concept, and that is inflation. How does inflation affect your dollar? (sec. 3)

Reinforcement can be used to build confidence in your students, as well as establish the culture of the classroom. Creating a culture will be discussed further in the next chapter, but you cannot just start firing higher level questions at students who might not be used to them. They might feel defensive or not want to participate due to lack of comfort. You have to make students feel as though your classroom is a safe place to answer questions—that answers, even wrong ones, are welcome and encouraged. Positive reinforcement is a good way to let students know your classroom is a safe environment.

Probing questions can push students to the next level of thinking. In the example given from CITL (n.d.), the instructor uses three probing question to develop more in-depth ideas. The instructor could have just stopped after the first question, but then he or she would not have gotten to the upper levels of Bloom's taxonomy. The first probing question merely takes the thinking to an application level, but the final probing question ratchets it up to an evaluating level. The rigor has been raised because the student not only has to give an answer, but also has to justify it. Probing questions are the quickest route to taking a dialogue with students into higher order thinking. You just have to make sure you are asking the right questions.

CITL (n.d.) also suggested that you adjust/refocus. This will challenge students a little more than reinforcement. Refocusing keeps students on track but also can take them to all sorts of interesting places. Notice that, in the example, instead of just correcting the student back to the original question, the instructor used the answer to take the conversation in another interesting direction. Just like the saying "sometimes the best trip is the one you didn't plan," sometimes the best thinking in a conversation happens when students get off of the beaten path and bring up seemingly unrelated topics. Although you do not want students to get too far off-topic, allowing them to explore certain avenues, even if it leads to a dead end, can produce a lot of higher order thinking.

RUNNING A DISCUSSION

This chapter has shared several strategies for raising the rigor of the verbal questions you ask in class. Verbal questions can be introduced during a one-on-one conversation with a student, when talking to groups, or during a whole-class discussion. The best way to involve the entire class is to have a discussion—a sharing of multiples ideas and thoughts. How do you manage all of your students and have a thought-provoking discussion that helps students learn?

You already know that good questioning is going to be the key factor in having an effective discussion. Before leading a discussion, you have to decide what you want the discussion to accomplish and then prepare questions that will help you get there. For instance, if the point of your discussion is to determine student knowledge and understanding, the discussion questions should focus on content. If you want to understand students' opinions, then you need to ask questions that call for students to provide them. If you want to raise the rigor in your classroom and dig a little deeper into a topic, then you will need questions in the upper levels of Bloom's to get kids thinking. There are a few things you can do to get in the proper frame of mind and lay the groundwork for a successful discussion (Yale Poorvu Center for Teaching and Learning, n.d.):

» **Communicate expectations:** If there is something you want to get out of a discussion, be up front with students about the goal. There should not be a hidden agenda. Students should be aware of what you are trying to accomplish so they can help you to get there.

» **Incorporate different teaching strategies:** A discussion does not need to look like the traditional method, in which the teacher stands at the front of the class asking a series of questions while students raise their hands, waiting to be called on. There are all sorts of different ways you can set up your discussion. You might have students break into smaller groups and provide them with some essential questions but allow them to run their own discussion. You could divide students into pairs to have a conversation with one another about the topic. You will want to provide guidance, but letting them have a casual conversation might allow them to explore things they would not be willing to if the entire class was involved. You could also pose questions and have students write responses for 5 minutes before beginning the discussion to give them time to process and think.

» **Be open-minded:** Sometimes a discussion will go somewhere you did not intend or expect it to. Sometimes you just need to allow students to explore something. This means they might take the discussion to a lot of dead ends, but the journey is the real learning experience. You have to be okay with things not going exactly as planned. Learning is messy, and discussions should be, too.

» **Do not be afraid to relinquish control:** Just because you are the teacher does not mean you have to be in control during the entire discussion. A successful discussion is one that you manage, not one that you dictate. Your questions should be designed to get students talking. If you are hearing yourself more than your student voices, then they might not be doing as much learning as you would like. You need to give up trying to find the perfect answer and accept the answers your students provide, adjusting when needed, but giving them some leeway to explore.

» **Be prepared:** The more prepared you are, the less chance something will go wrong. This may mean scripting questions out ahead of time. Be careful that you are not writing a script that you expect to be read line by line. It is perfectly fine to have more questions than you are going to use. In fact, it is preferable because that means the questions are garnering longer, deeper responses or are leading students to ask questions.

REFLECTION QUESTIONS

1. What kinds of questions do you verbally ask your students in your day-to-day classroom?
2. How much time do you spend preparing questions ahead of time?
3. How thoughtful are you about your follow-up questions? Are they designed to dig deeper?
4. Are you ready to lead a thought-provoking discussion? What can you do to prepare?

Chapter 9

Establishing a Rigorous Classroom Culture

Essential Question
Is your classroom a place where students feel safe to take risks in answering questions?

In order to get students comfortable with higher level questioning, a rigorous classroom culture needs to be established. This chapter details how to accomplish this feat, including how to set deliberate expectations of your students.

THE FIRST DAY OF SCHOOL

The first day of school is the one day of the year that every student is excited to be in class. Yet, students often passively sit in class on that day, listening to someone tell them what they can and cannot do. What if, instead, you started students off on the right foot and got them excited about the type of thinking they will be doing in your class?

One option is to start with an icebreaker that asks students higher level questions about themselves and the kinds of learners they are. This helps you get to know your students, and it gets them used to the types of open-ended questions you will be asking. Heick (2019) recommended the following 10 questions:

1. What do you love? What are you most proud of?
2. How do you respond—emotionally, practically, etc.— when you're challenged?
3. What do you need from me to be successful this year?
4. What does it mean to 'understand' something?
5. What should school 'do' for you?
6. What should you do with the things you learn?
7. What do you want to learn about this year? What are you curious about? What can a person do with curiosity?
8. When are you most creative? Why do you think that might be?
9. What do you want me to know about you? What should I be asking you but I'm not?
10. Do you think you're a good student? A good learner? Is there a difference?

Because students may be new to this level of thinking, you might want to give them these questions first and let them brainstorm and/or write about them. Then, you can have a discussion during which students get the chance to be active. Christensen (2017) outlined three suggestions for how you might set up this discussion:

» **Discussion Diamond:** Students are asked to respond to a statement or question and commit to the reasoning behind their point of view. Group members independently respond to the question or statement, jot down their thoughts, and then share their responses with the team. The group then develops a summary to share with the class. This strategy emphasizes respect, active listening, and critical thinking.

» **Four Corners Discussion:** Students choose a view or perspective on a statement or question and share their reasoning. This strategy gets students up and moving, as well as encourages listening, verbal communication, critical thinking, and decision making.

» **Talk Moves:** Students move away from the recitation style of discussion and into a more student-centered discussion format. Students are provided with basic prompts to be used in the classroom as follow-ups to questions, such as "Do you agree with [other student's] point of view?" or "Why do you think that?" or "Tell me more." (pp. 47–49).

Whichever strategy you choose, you want to establish that your classroom is a place where questions fly freely and students are expected to think.

FIRST POINT OF CONTACT

Another way to create a rigorous culture, as well as make connections with students, is by greeting your students as they come into class. Typically, you might greet students with a "Hello" or "How was your weekend?" These brief greetings and conversations are important. However, just like rigorous questions are needed in other areas in the classroom, there are better questions you can ask when greeting students. Here are five alternatives to ask students as they come into class, according to Ludema and Johnson (2019):

1. What was the best part about your day?
2. What work is most exciting you this week?
3. What new ideas are giving you energy lately?
4. Tell me one thing you've learned recently that inspired you.
5. What is one thing we could do right now to make this (day, project, event) even better? (para. 6)

These questions go beyond a simple greeting. They will be more time-consuming, as you will have to focus more on each student, but this is how you build relationships and establish trust with students.

Studies have shown that welcoming a student by name or with a positive greeting can increase student academic engagement by 20%, decreasing disruptive behavior by 9% (Cook et al., 2018). Imagine how much more you could increase this by not only greeting students, but also engaging with them. Doing so builds a sense of community and will help you form personal relationships with students. The result makes the relationship between student and teacher more casual than formal, which builds a questioning environment in which students feel safe asking and answering questions.

You can also hold a "Monday Contemplation Meeting" at the beginning of the week, during which, instead of focusing on content and academics, you focus on building relationships and a culture of questioning. The meeting only needs to last 10 to 15 minutes and center around a single question that you ask students to contemplate. Consider questions that are big picture and do not require a lot of background knowledge, but push students toward critical thinking. Think of these meetings as stretching before doing some athletic activity, only in this case you are stretching students' minds. Some contemplation meeting question ideas might include:

» If you could have any superpower, what would you choose?
» What gets in the way of you learning what you want to learn?

» What state or country do you want to travel to, and for what purpose?
» What is your favorite number, and why?
» If you had to eat one food for the rest of your life, what would it be?
» Describe your perfect day.
» What is a holiday you wish you could create, and why?
» Should kids get rewarded for getting good grades?
» Someone has given you a million dollars. What would you do with it?
» Why are pizzas round, cut into triangles, and put into square boxes?

You should ask questions that would be fun to pose, ponder, and explore. Do not facilitate the discussion—pose the question and see where students' thinking goes. The answers do not matter, although you can learn a lot about your students through their answers. What matters is that you are requiring them to access the deeper parts of their brains and to critically think. You are getting them warmed up for the higher level thinking that will be required in your classroom.

CHARACTERISTICS OF A THINKING CLASSROOM

Managing a classroom is probably the single greatest challenge for a teacher. When I am watching teachers new to the profession, rarely do they have a good grasp on how to manage their class. They are just trying to survive and learn on the job. Only after a few years of experience do many teachers begin to get the hang of classroom management. Even if you are a veteran teacher, there are always new and better ways to manage your classroom. If you are wanting to create a rigorous thinking culture in your classroom, there are a few elements you will want to have in your management system for you and students to follow (see Figure 14):

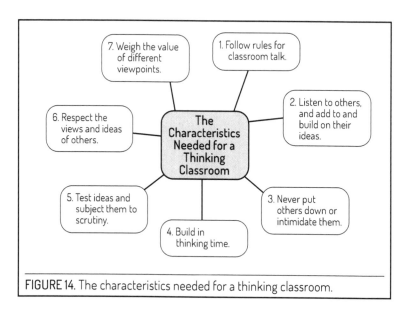

FIGURE 14. The characteristics needed for a thinking classroom.

1. **Follow rules for classroom talk:** You can decide how you want to establish rules for students talking in class. I have found the best way to do this is to create norms with your students so that everyone understands and respects the expectations. Creating norms together makes students more aware of the manner in which they should talk in class and causes them to care more because they helped create the norms (e.g., be respectful of others, participate, listen before talking, don't dominate the conversation, pay attention, etc.).

2. **Listen to others, and add to and build on their ideas:** Ideally, if you have set your classroom up as a thinking environment, students will be able to generate most of the higher level questions on their own. One way to do this is to teach students to listen to the ideas generated by fellow classmates and use them to build even deeper conversations. In practice, this type of environment might look something like the following conversation. Notice how the teacher does not speak at all during this exchange:

Student 1:	I think we should be making efforts to use more renewable resources, such as wind or the sun, in order to generate energy that is cleaner.
Student 2:	Are you aware of how expensive those things are?
Student 3:	And how much space they take up or how loud they are? My cousin lives across from a wind turbine, and he says it can be very noisy.
Student 1:	Isn't it worth it though? To have energy that is so much cleaner than oil and coal?
Student 3:	If they find a way to make it more efficient. Do you think they could do that?
Student 1:	Don't know, but I know cars used to be a whole lot louder, and with advancing technology they aren't so much anymore.
Student 2:	You still haven't addressed the expense.
Student 1:	I think once there are more renewable sources out there, the price will come down. Computers used to cost $5,000, but nowadays even faster and lighter ones are less than half the cost. Besides, I'd be willing to pay a little more now so that my great-great-grandchildren have access to energy sources because coal and oil are going to run out. That's why they're called nonrenewable.

3. **Never put others down or intimidate them:** You want to build an environment in which students feel safe talking in class. Any norms/rules should help with this, but you also need to be sure students are being respectful toward one another, no one is dominating the conversation, and everyone feels valued. This also applies to you as the teacher. I always find it amazing how much what we say influences the classroom. An offhanded remark here or a teasing comment there can shut a student down and make the student feel as though he or she is not welcome to par-

ticipate. That might not have been your intention, but all students should feel comfortable sharing their thoughts.

4. **Build in thinking time:** If you want students to think, then you need to provide time and space for them to do so. This means increasing your wait time for responses. Classroom questioning often involves a call and response. The teacher asks the question, the student with his or her hand up first shouts out the answer, and the teacher moves onto the next question. Consider this: When you ask a higher level question, do not let students raise their hands until at least a minute has passed. This allows students a chance to process the question and, in most cases, will result in a deeper, well-thought-out answer. You could even take this a step further and have students journal about an answer before verbally answering. This allows students the chance to capture their processing before turning it into an answer for public consumption. Answers are more likely to be well-thought-out and constructed because students were afforded the opportunity to think in more depth.

5. **Test ideas and subject them to scrutiny:** This is part of that risk-taking behavior you want students to be willing to try in your class. You want your students to voice big ideas that are not fully formed, or to challenge the status quo when you pose ideas. This means teaching students to dissent in a formal manner—that it is okay to disagree with someone, including the teacher, as long as they are respectful and as long as they are clear in their rationale for doing so. When a student shares a theory, make time for the class to put it under the microscope.

6. **Respect the views and ideas of others:** Students can begin to feel unsafe in classroom discussion when they feel that their views and ideas are not respected. Remind students to be respectful of others' views, but allow your students to decide their views for themselves. As the teacher, try to balance both sides of an argument and look at the issue from both points of view. If the teacher picks

a side, students from the other side are probably going to feel slighted. Whatever your beliefs about an issue, your job is to make sure students hear both sides of the issue and think for themselves. This is what raises the rigor in your classroom and creates thinkers. Some students will also feel very passionate about their side of the issue, and your role is not to judge their stance or to let others judge it, but to allow it to be heard, while fostering constructive discussion. This can be a tough balancing act but one that you will need to maintain so that students feel respected.

7. **Weigh the value of different viewpoints:** Again, consider all student voices, no matter how against your own principles they may be. Allowing students to voice their opinions leads to thought-provoking discussions. As much as possible you need to leave your own bias out of a lesson. You also have to help students see the value in weighing different viewpoints—that it is perfectly acceptable to believe what they believe, but they must be willing to listen to the other side before making their decisions.

STRATEGIES FOR ASKING AND RECEIVING QUESTIONS

Here are some strategies to consider in order to create a culture of thinking in your classroom. Many of these have already been addressed in earlier chapters, but here they are in one list for reference purposes:

» **Phrasing:** Communicate each question so that students understand the response expectation (McComas & Rossier, n.d.). If you ask a question that elicits a one- or two-word response, that is what you are going to get. For a written response, if you provide only a single line for students to write on, you'll get a one-sentence response. If you want layers and depth to student answers, your questions need to have those qualities as well.

» **Sequencing:** Ask questions in a patterned order, indicating a purposeful questioning strategy (McComas & Rossier, n.d.). Scaffold your questions. Start out by asking some lower level ones and then build up to higher level ones.

» **Balance:** Ask both lower and higher level questions, and balance the time between the two types (McComas & Rossier, n.d.). Use questions at an appropriate level or levels to achieve the objectives of the lesson. Remember, you typically want a 50:50 ratio of higher level to lower level questions. There will some lessons during which you will need to use a lot of lower level questions to determine understanding, but there should be others with more higher level questions if students are going into more depth with a topic.

» **Participation:** Use questions to stimulate a wide range of student participation, encouraging responses from all students—even those who have not volunteered to respond (McComas & Rossier, n.d.). Most students will not answer questions they do not find interesting. You need to ask questions that are so compelling that a student cannot help but want to participate. The traditional method of having students raise their hands and calling on the first to go up needs to be changed. In my classroom, I had a "no raised hands" policy. If students raised their hands, I would not call on them. Instead, the expectation was that everyone should be ready to answer any questions at any time. Because that was the expectation from the very first day of class, students were not caught off guard when I called on them. We developed safety nets, such as "ask a friend," and they could ask a fellow student to help them, or they could "take 5," and I would move on and come back to them in 5 minutes after they had had time to think about the question.

» **Unpacking:** Probe initial student answers, and encourage students to expand upon their answers (McComas & Rossier, n.d.). Do not let students off easy with their answers. Play the role of Socrates, asking follow-up questions to arrive at a deeper answer. I cannot tell you how many times I have observed a teacher, and a student gives a really intriguing answer, only to have the teacher just move on to the next student or question, missing the opportunity to unpack the student's response. Take advantage of these moments—ask for further clarification or justification for the answer.

» **Wait time:** Pause for a few seconds after asking a question to allow students time to think. Also pause after students' initial responses to questions (McComas & Rossier, n.d.). If you want your students to be thinkers, you have to give them time to think. There are many different types of thinkers. Some students hear a question and can instantly come up with a pretty thoughtful response. There are others who like to consider questions in more depth until they are able to formulate a coherent response. Their answer might be just as, if not more profound, than the quick thinkers, but you may never get to hear these thoughts if you are too busy moving on to the next question. You need to provide opportunities for these thoughtful processers to be able to participate.

GETTING YOUR STUDENTS TO ASK THE QUESTIONS THEMSELVES

The ultimate goal is to be able to take your higher level questioning abilities and pass them on to your students. This involves setting up your classroom as a place where asking higher level questions is an everyday occurrence and students are comfortable with them.

How can you tell if your students have become critical thinkers? The following list of characteristics will help you decide:

1. Independently ask pertinent questions.
2. Reason, analyze and weigh statements and arguments.

3. Have a sense of curiosity and wonder, being interested in finding out, new information or solutions.
4. Can define criteria for analyzing ideas and problems.
5. Are willing to examine beliefs, challenge assumptions and opinions, weigh them against facts (distinguishing between fact, opinion, bias and prejudice).
6. Listen respectfully and carefully to others so that they are able to give feedback.
7. Suspend judgment until all facts have been gathered and considered.
8. Looks for evidence to support assumption and beliefs.
9. Are able and flexible enough to adjust opinions when new facts are found.
10. Examines problems closely and looks for proof.
11. Able to identify and reject information that is incorrect or irrelevant.
12. Make assertions based on sound logic and solid evidence.
13. Able to admit a lack of understanding or information.
14. Recognizes that critical thinking is a lifelong process of self-assessment. (as cited in Gast, n.d., p. 14)

You can cultivate creative thinkers by leading by example and asking higher level questions whenever the opportunity arises. Also provide a safe environment in which it is not only permissible to ask questions, but encouraged as well. This will give your students the space to ask higher level questions. There are also a few additional strategies you can use to encourage students to ask their own questions:

1. **Have students prepare questions ahead of discussions:** When you have a discussion coming up, have students generate questions ahead of time. Students can then lead and be more invested in the discussion.
2. **Have students run their own smaller discussions:** You do not need to be the overseer of all discussions in class. Dividing students into smaller groups and allowing them to run their own discussions will help them build independence toward creating their own questions. As you

start implementing this strategy, you might have a sheet of paper with a few starter questions, but then let students take over the conversation.

3. **Provide students with a place on assessments for asking any questions they are pondering:** Students are rarely provided with space to ask their own questions that might crop up when they are pondering your questions on assessments. What if you provided a space where students could pose their questions? Then, you can either address the questions on their test, or maybe collect students' questions for a classroom discussion.

4. **Give students ample opportunities to bring up questions when reflecting upon their learning:** Provide students with opportunities to reflect. Essential questions or other protocols to allow them to explore their thoughts and feelings can be very valuable in determining what they truly learned. It can also be valuable to give them a space to share questions that might have come up during reflection. You could create a bulletin board or section of the white board where students can pose their questions—anonymously or labeled with their name. When you get enough questions, you can dedicate some class time to talking about the questions and hear everyone's thoughts.

Anything you can do to provide a rigorous learning environment and specifically train students in asking good questions will benefit them not only in school, but also for the rest of their lives. Keep in mind that there a few things you need to make sure you consider for your classroom environment (Buono, n.d.):

» Designing higher order questions requires planning time.
» Responding to higher order questions requires a low-risk environment.
» Responding to higher order questions requires extended think and wait time.
» Students should be taught and expected to ask each other higher order questions.

» All students should be engaged in asking and responding to questions.

REFLECTION QUESTIONS

1. What can you do to ensure your classroom is a safe environment for students to think?
2. What is one thing you could do right now to make your classroom an environment where higher level thinking takes place?
3. Does the higher level thinking permeate all of your classroom activities, or does it feel like an add-on? How can you build it into all aspects of your classroom?
4. How many of the six strategies for asking and receiving questions do you do fairly regularly in your classroom?
5. Do you expect your students to ask as many thought-provoking questions as you expect of yourself? How do/can you help students accomplish this?

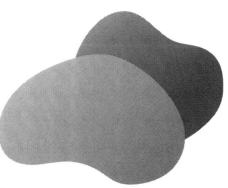

Conclusion

Raising the rigor in your classroom means changing your teaching practices. This is not to say that you were never challenging your students before. Now, however, you are equipped with a strong awareness of how often you are challenging students. This book has provided you with strategies to collect data to understand your classroom questioning practices and the tools to make improvements.

Building awareness of my questioning practices transformed my teaching. Previously, I may have employed a 5:95 ratio of higher level to lower level questions in my classroom. Becoming more aware of the types of questions I asked and how I was asking them helped me move toward a 50:50 ratio, and I have definitely seen the rigor increase in my classes as a result.

I have a few pieces of parting advice from my experiences. As you set up a classroom in which it is acceptable for students to fail, remember that you, too, should be afforded the same opportunity. There are going to be times when a discussion does not go as planned or students do not perform well on an assessment you wrote. Your willingness to admit and take ownership of mistakes and learn from them shows students that failure is okay and can be overcome.

Second, never take the easy way out—it only cheats your students. Poor teaching, in most cases, is a result of taking the easy way. A teacher may not want to grade 150 essays so he provides his students with a quick multiple-choice assessment, even though he knows the multiple-choice questions will not assess for mastery as well as the written responses. Writing well-thought-out higher level questions is much more difficult than giving students lower level, rote memorization questions, but higher level questions are best for your learners.

My third piece of advice is to follow the three rules to spark learning developed by Ramsey Musallam (2013). He said we should confuse our students, perplex them, and evoke real questions in them because student questions are the seeds of real learning. He created three rules that he successfully used to change his teaching:

1. Curiosity comes first.
2. Embrace the mess.
3. Practice reflection.

That leads into my fourth piece of advice: Continue to reflect on your practice. If you ever get to the point in your teaching career where you say, "I've got this now," then you are doing something wrong. You will never "get this now" because teaching is not made up of widgets and programs—human beings are constantly evolving and changing. Teaching is like life. Every time you think you have figured out, you'll likely discover there is something else you could be doing better. If you are teaching correctly, you will feel uncomfortable for 30-plus years, or however long you spend in the classroom.

Look back at the essential questions that started each chapter. See if your initial responses have changed from what you learned in this book. If your thoughts have changed, then I have accomplished what I hoped to with this book. I hope you are thinking more in depth about your teaching and questioning practices. I hope you raise the rigor in your classroom. I hope you do what is best for your students.

References

Abla, C., & Maxfield, L. (2017). Higher-order questioning inspires higher-level thinking. *McRel International*. Retrieved from https://www.mcrel.org/higher-order-questioning-inspires-higher-level-thinking

Aishwarya.gudadhe. (2015). *A map of how divergent thinking works.* Retrieved from https://en.wikipedia.org/wiki/Divergent_thinking#/media/File:Final_divergent_thinking.jpg

Anderson, L., & Krathwohl, D. R. (Eds.). (2001). *A taxonomy for learning, teaching, and assessing: A revision of Bloom's taxonomy of educational objectives* (Complete ed.). New York, NY: Longman.

Anderson, L. W., & Sosniak, L. A. (Eds). (1994). *Bloom's taxonomy: A forty-year retrospective.* Chicago, IL: National Society for the Study of Education.

Bisol, J. L. (2015). *An ostentation of tutoring.* Author.

Bloom, B. (Ed.). (1956). *Taxonomy of educational objectives: The classification of educational goals. Handbook I: Cognitive domain.* New York, NY: Longmans Green.

Brulles, D., & Brown, K. L. (2018). *A teacher's guide to flexible grouping and collaborative learning: Form, manage, assess, and differentiate in groups.* Minneapolis, MN: Free Spirit.

Buono, S. (n.d.). *Developing higher order thinking questions to promote student learning* [PowerPoint slides]. Retrieved from http://www.palmyraschools.com/ps/Departments/Curriculum%20and%20Instruction/Professional%20Development/Higher%20Order%20Thinking%20Presentation.pdf

Busteed, B. (2013). The school cliff: Student engagement drops with each school year. *Gallup.* Retrieved from https://news.gallup.com/opinion/gallup/170525/school-cliff-student-engagement-drops-school-year.aspx

Butler, H. A., Pentoney, C., & Bong, M. P. (2017). Predicting real-world outcomes: Critical thinking ability is a better predictor of life decisions than intelligence. *Thinking Skills and Creativity, 25,* 38–46.

Cardellichio, T., & Field, W. (1997). Seven strategies that encourage neural branching. *Educational Leadership, 54*(6), 33–36.

Center for Innovation in Teaching & Learning, University of Illinois. (n.d.). *Questioning strategies.* Retrieved from https://citl.illinois.edu/citl-101/teaching-learning/resources/teaching-strategies/questioning-strategies

Center for Learning, Vanderbilt University. (2016). *Bloom's taxonomy.* Retrieved from https://www.flickr.com/photos/vandycft/29428436431

Christensen, C. L. (2017). What is the impact of effective questioning and critical, relevant conversations on sixth grade science students' agentic engagement? *School of Education Student Capstone Theses and Dissertations.* 4307.

Cook, C. R., Fiat, A., Larson, M., Daikos, C., Slemrod, T., Holland, E. A., . . . Renshaw, T. (2018). Positive greetings at the door: Evaluation of a low-cost, high-yield proactive classroom management strategy. *Journal of Positive Behavior Interventions, 20,* 149–159.

Costa, A. L., & Kallick, B. (Eds.). (2008). *Learning and leading with habits of mind: 16 essential characteristics for success.* Alexandria, VA: Association for Supervision and Curriculum Development.

Cox, J. (n.d.). Teaching strategies that enhance higher order thinking. *TeachHUB.* Retrieved from https://www.teachhub.com/teaching-strategies-enhance-higher-order-thinking

Edward R. Murrow High School. (n.d.). *Costa's three levels of questioning.* Retrieved from https://www.ermurrowhs.org/uploads/6/2/6/8/6268393/costas-questioning-14.pdf

Fusco, E. (2012). *Effective questioning strategies in the classroom: A step-by-step approach to engaged thinking and learning, K–8.* New York, NY: Teachers College Press.

Gallagher, J. J., & Aschner, M. J. (1963). A preliminary report on analyses of classroom interaction. *Merrill-Palmer Quarterly, 9,* 183–194.

Gast, G. (n.d.). *Effective questioning and classroom talk: To develop learning & higher order thinking, promoting imagination, speculation, creative thinking & to pitch a suitable challenge level.* Retrieved from http://www.nsead.org/downloads/Effective_Questioning&Talk.pdf

Great Schools Partnership. (2014). Rigor. *The Glossary of Education Reform for Journalists, Parents, and Community Members.* Retrieved from https://www.edglossary.org/rigor

Hattie, J. (2018). Hattie ranking: 252 influences and effect sizes related to student achievement. *Visible Learning.* Retrieved from https://visible-learning.org/hattie-ranking-influences-effect-sizes-learning-achievement

Heick, T. (2019). 12 questions to ask your students on the first day of school. *Teach Thought.* Retrieved from https://www.teachthought.com/pedagogy/12-questions-ask-students-first-day-school

Jaeger, S. (n.d.). *Question generator*. Retrieved from https://www. sethjaeger.com/p/question-generator.html

Levy, J., & Sidhu, P. (2013). In the US, 21st century skills linked to word success: Real-world problem-solving most strongly tied to work quality. *Gallup*. Retrieved from https://news.gallup. com/poll/162818/21st-century-skills-linked-work-success. aspx

Ludema, J. & Johnson, A. (2018). Five questions you can ask instead of "how are you?" *Forbes*. Retrieved from https://www.forbes. com/sites/amberjohnson-jimludema/2018/04/05/five-questions-you-can-ask-instead-of-how-are-you/#68da19d49 683

McComas, W. F., & Rossier, L. A. (n.d.). *Asking more effective questions*. Retrieved from https://uwaterloo.ca/centre-for-teaching-excellence/sites/ca.centre-for-teaching-excellence/files/ uploads/files/asking_better_questions.pdf

Mississippi Department of Education. (2009). *Webb's depth of kno-wledge guide: Career and technical education definitions*. Retrieved from https://www.aps.edu/sapr/documents/ resources/Webbs_DOK_Guide.pdf

Msingh209. (2012). *A map of how convergent thinking works*. Retrieved from https://en.wikipedia.org/wiki/Convergent_ thinking#/media/File:Map_of_Convergent_Thinking.jpg

Musallam, R. (2013). 3 rules to spark learning [Video file]. *TED*. Retrieved from https://www.ted.com/talks/ramsey_ musallam_3_rules_to_spark_learning/details?nolanguage=en

National Governors Association Center for Best Practices, & Council of Chief State School Officers. (2010a). *Common Core State Standards for English language arts*. Washington, DC: Author.

National Governors Association Center for Best Practices, & Council of Chief State School Officers. (2010b). *Common Core State Standards for mathematics*. Washington, DC: Author.

NGSS Lead States. (2013). *Next generation science standards: For states, by states*. Washington, DC: The National Academies Press.

Northern Indiana ESC. (n.d.). *Depth of knowledge (DOK) overview chart*. Retrieved from http://www.niesc.k12.in.us/index. cfm/staff-development/public-consulting-group-co-teaching-session/depthofknowledgechart-pdf

Partnership for 21st Century Skills. (2011). *Framework for 21st century learning*. Washington, DC: Author.

Scholastic. (n.d.). *What makes paper airplanes fly?* Retrieved from https://www.scholastic.com/teachers/articles/teaching-content/what-makes-paper-airplanes-fly

Smart, J. B., & Marshall, J. C. (2012). Interactions between classroom discourse, teacher questioning and student cognitive engagement in middle school science. *Science Teacher Education, 24,* 249–267.

Smith, H., & Wentworth, M. (2019). Chalk talk. *School Reform Initiative*. Retrieved from https://www.schoolreforminitiative. org/download/chalk-talk

The Teacher Toolkit. (n.d.). *Exit ticket*. Retrieved from http://www.theteachertoolkit.com/index.php/tool/exit-ticket

Webb, N. L. (1997). *Criteria for alignment of expectations and assessments in mathematics and science education*. Research Monograph No. 6. Madison, WI: National Institute for Science Education.

Webb, N. L. (2002). *Depth-of-knowledge levels for four content areas*. Retrieved from http://ossucurr.pbworks.com/w/file/fetch/49691156/Norm%20web%20dok%20by%20subject%20area.pdf

Woodford, C. (2019). Airplanes. *Explain That Stuff*. Retrieved from https://www.explainthatstuff.com/howplaneswork.html

Yale Poorvu Center for Teaching and Learning. (n.d.) *Leading discussion*. Retrieved from https://poorvucenter.yale.edu/teaching/teaching-how/chapter-2-teaching-successful-section/leading-discussion

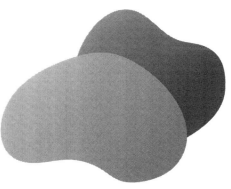

About the Author

Todd Stanley is the author of many teacher education books, including *Project-Based Learning for Gifted Students: A Handbook for the 21st-Century Classroom*, *Authentic Learning: Real-World Experiences That Build 21st-Century Skills*, and *Using Rubrics for Performance-Based Assessment: A Practical Guide to Evaluating Student Work*. He was a classroom teacher for 18 years, teaching students as young as second graders and as old as high school seniors, and was a National Board Certified teacher. He is currently gifted services coordinator for Pickerington Local School District, OH, where he lives with his wife, Nicki, and two daughters, Anna and Abby. You can follow Todd on Twitter @the_gifted_guy, or you can visit his website at https://www.thegiftedguy.com, where there are many free resources available, including blogs, professional development video tutorials, and classroom materials.